*To **Misha** and **AmiLove**,*
custody kids who experienced
all five stages and nonetheless
reached their adulthoods with
wisdom and beauty.

CHILD CUSTODY EVALUATIONS

UNDERSTANDING THE FIVE STAGES OF CUSTODY

S*by*OCIAL WORKERS

KEN LEWIS

NASW PRESS

National Association of Social Workers
Washington, DC

James J. Kelly, PhD, ACSW, LCSW, *President*
Elizabeth J. Clark, PhD, ACSW, MPH, *Executive Director*

Cheryl Y. Bradley, *Publisher*
Lisa M. O'Hearn, *Managing Editor*
Sarah Lowman, *Senior Editor*
Louise R. Goines, *Copyeditor*
Juanita Ruffin, *Proofreader*
Karen Schmitt, *Indexer*

Cover design by Metadog Design Group
Interior design by Xcel Graphic Services, Inc.
Printed and bound by Victor Graphics, Inc.

Library of Congress Cataloging-in-Publication Data

Lewis, Ken, 1941–
    Child custody evaluations by social workers : understanding the five stages of
custody / Ken Lewis.
        p. cm.
    ISBN 978-0-87101-387-3
    1. Custody of children—United States—Evaluation.   2. Social workers—
Legal status, laws, etc.—United States.   3. Evidence, Expert—United States.
I. Title.

KF547.L49   2009
362.82'9430973—dc22

                                                                    2009017718

Printed in the United States of America

Contents

Introduction

S ocial work is a dynamic profession that at its core helps individuals, families, and communities solve problems. Social workers in the United States have long been involved in legal issues. For example, in the late 19th and early 20th centuries, Jane Addams was heavily involved in the legal issues of her day: rights of immigrant children, right to voice antiwar protests, and right for women to vote. Through the years, according to Susan Brooks (cited in Govern, 2004), "a lot of the principles, values and theories . . . that social work has adopted as a field have come to influence the law" (p. 4).

Brooks contrasted traditional family law, with its emphasis on blame and punishment, with the therapeutic approaches emerging in family law, including mediation and court-ordered family therapy.

There is nothing antithetical between social work and the law. Social workers care about the well-being of families, and because of their training and experience, social workers can offer valuable services to family courts, particularly in matters of contested child custody.

When mediation, conciliation, and other efforts to resolve a child custody dispute fail, the case goes to court. But how does the judge make a determination of what is best for the child, and how does the judge determine whether or not mental health intervention would benefit the child?

Family court judges across the country have long welcomed partnerships with mental health professionals to help resolve custody disputes. In the southwest, New Mexico's former presiding family court judge Ann Kass (1998) wrote:

Legal professionals and mental health professionals working together in custody disputes have enormous potential to do good. . . . I believe it is essential for these two professions to work to forge new partnerships in helping families resolve custody disputes more effectively and more humanely. (p. 257)

In the east, the same sentiment was expressed by a New Jersey appellate judge in *Fehnel v. Fehnel* (1982) when he wrote about the difficulty that judges have in custody cases, and how experts might help:

There are obviously few judicial tasks which involve the application of greater sensitivity, delicacy and discretion than the adjudication of child custody disputes, which result in greater impact on the lives of those affected by the adjudication, and which require a higher degree of attention to the properly considered views of professionals in other disciplines. That is why . . . the parties must be afforded every reasonable opportunity to introduce expert witnesses whose evaluation of the family situation may assist the judge in determining what is best for the children. (186 N.J. Super. at 212, 452 A.2d at 215)

In the northwest, one statute allows a judge to order the parents to consult with "an appropriate professional":

The court may, at any time, direct the parties to consult with appropriate professionals for the purpose of assisting the parties to formulate a plan for implementation of the custody order or to resolve any controversy that has arisen in the implementation of a plan for custody. (Mont. Code Ann. § 40-4-224(4) 2007)

Many years ago, a South Carolina family court judge wrote about his desire to work in partnership with "knowledgeable professionals":

I too, earnestly desire a partnership. In a case of first impression, nothing pleases me more than to have knowledgeable professionals guide me as to where I should place children. Too often we judges must make these decisions almost alone. (personal communication with Hon. L. M. Rivers, Jr., March 1982)

The usefulness of a custody evaluation conducted by an expert has even been recognized in one state's rules.[1] The field of custody evaluations has been developing over the years, and social workers have played a major role across the country. Social workers in many states have been appointed as custody evalua-

---

[1]In Pennsylvania: "in order to make a proper determination in a child custody case, the court often requires information which can only be supplied by an expert evaluation of the parties and the subject child" (Pa. R. Civ. P. § 1915.8, Explanatory Comment, (1994)).

tors by the courts (see Appendix A). This field continues to be ripe for social workers who want to advocate for the child's best interests:

- Who better than a well-trained social worker could conduct a custody evaluation that would guide the judge in making custody and visitation determinations?
- Is it not the case that many social workers have the skills by training and by experience to become excellent guides?
- What are the essential segments of a custody evaluation, and what specific social work skills are needed at each step?

SEGMENTS OF A CUSTODY EVALUATION

Although each custody case is different, most evaluations include the procedures as shown in the following chart.

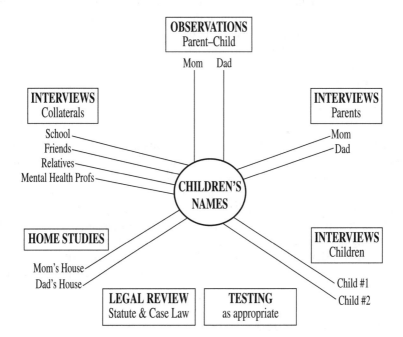

Interviewing

Interviewing should be a skill familiar to social workers. In custody evaluation work, interviews should be limited to those factors that have a bearing on what will be your recommendation for custody and visitation. In other words, you probably do not need to know much about a parent's high school experiences. It should be less important to understand how the parents functioned in their families of origin and more important to understand how the parents operated with their children during their marital life. It should be important to know the current beliefs that each parent holds about his or her own parenting strengths and weaknesses and the strengths and weaknesses of the other parent. "Thin slicing," as an interviewing technique, can be defined as the art of seeking the most information from the fewest questions (see Gladwell, 2005; Marsden, 2005).

In addition to the parents, interviews should be conducted with older children, family members, neighbors, school teachers, doctors, and others. Other interviews might be conducted with reference people whose names are provided by the parents. When there are conflicting renditions about important events, get them confirmed or denied by the reference people.

Observation

Observation is often the weakest segment for psychologists. They often rely more on testing than on direct observation of the parent–child interaction. Personality testing might be useful in clinical work, but for custody work, it has much less value than observation. Observing the parent–child interaction should provide the social worker with significant understanding of the child, which is not available by testing.

Home Study

Going to the proposed custodial home is an important segment of a custody evaluation, but it is frequently underrated and often omitted. The custody evaluator might find it valuable to observe where the child lives—see the yard, the basement play area, the child's bedroom, and the neighborhood. "Observing firsthand the physical, social, and emotional environments that each parent offers the child" (Skafte, 1985, p. 73) can provide valuable insight. A comparative home study might bring the evaluator closer to the child's own experiences. An office setting may be appropriate for administering tests and interviewing the mother and father, but a comparative home study will often provide crucial information unobtainable in an office setting.

Custody: Statutory and Case Law

Reading child custody law is not difficult, but it is the most forgotten segment in many custody evaluations. It is important to understand the law of custody in the jurisdiction where the evaluation is being conducted because legal presumptions and burdens of proof differ throughout the country. The importance of this has been recognized, for example, in the guidelines for social workers propagated by the Oregon Chapter of the National Association of Social Workers (NASW)

(2005) and the Louisiana State Board of Social Work Examiners (1998)—Oregon: "Knowledge of Statutes: The evaluator shall be familiar with the statutes and case law governing child custody" (Standard II-C); Louisiana: "The social worker should enhance his or her competency through specialized continuing education . . . [in] legal standards and procedures" (Guideline II-C).

The importance of knowing custody statutes and case law has also been included in the standards and guidelines published by other professional organizations:

- The psychologist also strives to become familiar with applicable legal standards and procedures, including laws governing divorce and custody adjudications in his or her state or jurisdiction. (American Psychological Association, 1994, Guideline 5-A)
- Evaluators shall be familiar with the applicable statutes, case law, and local rules governing child custody. These will vary from jurisdiction to jurisdiction, and evaluators must be knowledgeable concerning the criteria for original determination of custody, criteria for change of custody . . . (Association of Family and Conciliation Courts, 2006, Guideline 2.1(a), p. 74)
- The evaluator should know basic family law and legal procedures in his or her state, including the statutory and case law criteria that the courts use to determine custody. (American Academy of Child and Adolescent Psychiatry, 1997, p. 9)

Some states' custody provisions are spread across several statutes (for example, Massachusetts and Nevada) and other states (for example, Texas and Florida) have consolidated their custody laws. (For the location of custody statutes for every state, see Appendix B).

Some states have statutory custody factors (for example, Florida[2] and Minnesota[3]) and some states do not. In those states without statutory factors (for example, Pennsylvania[4] and North Carolina[5]), published appellate opinions (called case law) can guide the evaluator. Case law can be found on the Web sites of most state appellate courts or in the law libraries of many courthouses. Soon after their appointments, some evaluators ask the attorneys on both sides of the

---

[2]Fla. Stat., § 61.13(3).

[3]Minn. Stat. § 518.17 subdivision 1.

[4]Pennsylvania custody factors include "all factors that legitimately affect the child's physical, intellectual, moral, and spiritual well-being" (see, *K.B. v. C.B.F.*, 833 A.2d 767 at 776 (Pa. Super. 2003)).

[5]North Carolina's "primary concern is the furtherance of the welfare and best interests of the child and its placement in the home environment that will be most conducive to the full development of its physical, mental and moral faculties. All other factors . . . will be deferred or subordinated to these considerations" (see, *Evans v. Evans*, 138 N.C. App. 135 at 141; 530 E.E.2d 576 at 580 (2000), quoting *Griffith v. Griffith*, 240 N.C. 271 at 275; 81 S.E.2d 918 at 921 (1954)).

case to identify those custody factors that they find most important from the perspective of their side of the case.

Social workers conducting custody evaluations should become familiar with the statutory and case law factors in the jurisdiction in which the evaluation is being conducted. Although states have different factors, some of the more typical statutory and case law factors include the following:

- parents' desires for custody and access
- wishes expressed by the child, particularly the older child
- nature of the child's relationship with the parents and other significant people (for example, extended family)
- each parent's capacity to care for and provide for the emotional, intellectual, educational, medical, and welfare needs of the child
- child's maturity, sex, background (including culture), and religion
- home, school, and community history of the child
- mental, emotional, and physical health of each party
- moral fitness of each party insofar as it affects the welfare of the child
- willingness and ability of each party to facilitate and encourage a close and continuing relationship between the child and the other party
- conditions of the proposed custodial environments and the age-dependent suitability of the homes for the child
- continuity of existing parent–child attachments
- parents' attitudes and comparative parenting skills
- distance between the respective residences of the parties.

SKILLS NEEDED FOR THE CUSTODY EVALUATOR

The skills a social worker needs to conduct an effective comprehensive child custody evaluation can best be explained by the LEARN paradigm:

- *Listen.* Many people listen, not with their ears, but with what is behind their ears, in other words, their personal perception of something they hear; try to avoid that; keep an open mind. Develop the art of asking only those questions whose answers will provide relevant data for your task.
- *Eyes.* Many people see, not with their eyes, but with what is behind their eyes, in other words, their personal interpretation of something they see, or what you think you see is often influenced by what you expect to see. Try to avoid that. Watch especially carefully the parent–child interactions and be cognizant that most knowledge is influenced by the standpoint of the knower.
- *Assessment.* Use multiple sources for collecting data and see if certain themes develop from the data, then assess the data or themes in terms of what is relevant for the specific issues in the case.

- ***Recommend.*** Custody recommendations should be directly connected to the assessment of the data and themes. When developing an opinion from your data, identify what data underlie that opinion; be able to defend point by point what you recommend.
- ***Notes.*** Keep accurate and complete notes. If you issue a custody report and the case does not settle, you may be called as an expert to testify in court. Your complete notes may be subject to discovery by both sides in the case.

SOCIAL WORKERS MAKE GOOD CUSTODY EVALUATORS

How can it be argued that social workers can make good custody evaluators? Four reasons come to mind, and the skeleton of the argument, in question format, is as follows:

- Can a social worker understand the nature of marital discord?
- Can a social worker view a child's interconnectedness to his or her family?
- Can a social worker understand how a child feels?
- Can a social worker identify the specific therapeutic interventions that may be needed in a high-conflict case?

Now, these four skeleton questions are elaborated upon as follows:

- *Understanding the nature of marital discord.* Marital discord is a primary arena for the clinical social worker. Those social workers with experience in this area know this is a period of heightened dysfunction between people who previously shared trust, intimacy, and love. Experience with family members at the marital discord stage would be an excellent prelude to success in custody evaluation work.
- *Family interconnectedness.* Social workers understand that a child can be assessed not merely as an individual, but also as an important member of a family or even an extended family. Although the legal dictum in child custody is "the child's best interests," the individual child's interests are connected to, and sometimes even dependent upon, the interests of the reconstructed family. Because social work education includes knowledge of system theory,[6] the social worker conducting a custody evaluation can

---

[6]System theory was first introduced over 50 years ago: Ludwig von Bertalanffy, "General System Theory—A New Approach to Unity of Science," 23 *Human Biology* 303–361, December 1951. For its application to social work, see Julia M. Norlin and Wayne A. Chess, *Human Behavior and the Social Environment: Social Systems Theory* (Boston: Allyn & Bacon, 1997).

obtain significant data concerning the child's interrelatedness to other people.

- *Understanding how the child feels.* It should not be difficult for a social worker to understand custody does not mean the child is divorced from one of his or her parents. It merely means that there will be a rearrangement from the previous family structure. But sometimes children of divorce and separation do not understand this, and the social worker may be in an excellent position to "feel" what the child is feeling. After all, the child is the most crucial part of a child custody evaluation.

Research on children of divorce and separation indicates the following:

  – The impact of divorce can be more damaging for boys than girls.
  – Generally, older children appear to experience fewer developmental problems than younger children.
  – Preschoolers are most likely to revert to earlier behaviors, like toilet training problems, or excessive clinging.
  – Children ages five to eight are more likely to show common signs of grieving, like crying or sighing a lot, or retreating from the world.
  – Older pre-teens are frightened by the divorce, angry at the initiator of the divorce, and often worry about growing up without support from the whole family.
  – Adolescents may show signs of depression, act out inappropriately, and worry about experiencing marital and sexual failure in their own lives.
  – All family members seem to get worse before they get better. One study indicated the impact dwindles away within a year or two. Another study, though, indicated that after five years, one-third of the children were fine, one-third seemed to be muddling through, and one-third were looking back to their pre-divorce life with intense longing.[7]

- *Identifying specific therapeutic interventions for high-conflict case.*[8] A trained and experienced social worker should be in a good position to identify specific therapeutic interventions that might be needed in a high-conflict case. Furthermore, the social worker, as a member of the local professional community, might be in the best possible position to recommend a therapist who would be qualified in the area of intervention that the custody evaluator identifies.

---

[7]Elliot A. Fisch, "Children and Divorce," NASW, http://www.education.com/reference/article/Ref_Children_Divorce.

[8]Definitions of a high-conflict case differ, but the definition under a Texas statute provides a good working understanding: "'High-conflict case' means a suit affecting the parent–child relationship in which the parties demonstrate a pattern of (a) repetitive litigation; (b) anger and distrust; (c) difficulty in communicating about and cooperating in the care of their children" (Tex. Fam. Code § 153.601 (2008)).

FIVE STAGES OF CUSTODY

There is a popular belief in the general community that child custody is a one-time event, connected with divorce, and then over. In fact, there are five stages of custody, each with relatively clear time dimensions, and each calling for different social work skills. Chapters 1 through 5 describe each stage and provide examples of how the involvement of a social worker can provide invaluable help to the children and families involved. Making custody recommendations is an area of practice that clinical social workers are encountering in ever-increasing numbers (Luftman, Veltkamp, Clark, Lannacone, & Snooks, 2005). Social workers who already conduct evaluations will find this book useful, and those just beginning to conduct evaluations will find a format to follow.

The five stages of custody are marital discord, initial custody, visitation denial, custody modification, and child removal. With the exception of the first stage, the stages are opportunities for social workers to be appointed as custody evaluators. However, it would be advisable to have experience in the initial custody stage before taking an assignment in any of the subsequent stages.

Chapters 1 through 5 discuss each stage in terms of its definition and time frame, and the scope of intervention for social workers and lawyers. Also, case examples and techniques of intervention are offered for each stage. Finally, although definitions of each stage can be considered uniform around the country, the language of custody is different in different states. Therefore, whenever possible, this book uses the generic language of custody to be more easily read.

1

Marital Discord Stage

DEFINITION AND TIME FRAME

Marital discord can be defined as that period during a marriage when the couple experiences conflict in their relationship. It is noted for a lack of harmony and agreement on matters of importance to the couple. Communication is strained; shared experiences are few or nil; tenderness and respect are absent. The children are often aware of the tension between their parents but usually do not understand it. Sometimes the couple physically separates; often they consider it.

The time frame for the marital discord stage of custody is any time from the beginning of parenthood to the filing for divorce, separation, or initial custody. In some marriages, the couple may experience several periods of discord; in others, only one. Given that the present divorce rate is nearly 50 percent, it would be fair to conclude that marital discord is a common experience in family life today.

SOCIAL WORK INTERVENTION

The scope of social work intervention at this stage will focus on marital counseling, family therapy, family mediation, and the like. Here, the role of the social worker is to work with the family members to discover the underlying causes of the discord and to either repair what is weak or assist them in rearranging their various relationships through custody counseling, custody mediation, or both. If custody is subsequently litigated, the social worker may be called to present expert testimony.[9]

Traditionally, social work intervention at the marital discord stage was considered successful only when marital reconciliation had been achieved and the family had returned to a relatively stable state of equilibrium, at least on the surface. But the appearance of homeostasis does not necessarily mean a mentally healthy family. Modern practitioners know that it is sometimes better to dissolve the marriage and rearrange the patterns of association than to encourage the family to remain intact for appearances only.

Social scientists who study the phenomenon find that marital discord is rising rapidly; that it creates severe stress for many individuals; and that it is often responsible for psychiatric disorders, suicide, homicide, and a host of other deepseated mental disorders.

It has long been known that marital discord affects all family members (see Goode, 1956). Separation from spouse or child is reported to be the time of greatest stress in the marital discord period. Although couples without children often have a need for human services intervention during marital discord, there is an even greater need for helping professionals when there are children involved.

CASE EXAMPLES

Case examples of the marital discord stage are numerous and are composed of ingredients quite familiar to most married people. The following two examples are typical cases that are ripe for mental health intervention.

The Affair

Mother and father have been married for 16 years. They have two daughters, ages 13 and 11. In the early years of their marriage, they were active in many social activities and community organizations. Over the years, these associations kept the couple apart frequently. Last year, the father developed a relationship with a woman he met at a political rally, and they had an affair. Mother learned about it from a friend of hers and became very angry, first with her husband and then with herself. She became intolerable around the house—screaming at her husband and acting unreasonably with her children.

Father finally moved into an apartment for what he said would be a trial month. First, the two daughters began visiting him on weekends—then during the week. By the third month, the girls were spending 90 percent of their free

---

[9]See Firmin v. Firmin, 770 So.2d 930 (La. App. 2000) where the clinical social worker who had worked with both parents prior to the divorce presented expert testimony and "opined that Mr. Firmin could handle an equal custody arrangement" (770 So.2d at 935).

time with him. He began to enjoy the single-father lifestyle and liked the attention he was getting from his daughters. When the mother would call on the phone to speak with her daughters, she would sometimes cry after hanging up. She felt her whole life had fallen apart. She wanted to forgive and forget about the affair, but she did not know how to express this to her husband.

Mother went to a social worker for help. The social worker had three sessions with her and then invited the father to the fourth session. He came quite willingly. At this session, the couple decided to live apart for six months and try to become friends again. They even joked about dating each other. The social worker suggested the couple seek legal assistance to work out an arrangement for seeing the children during the next six months. The couple sought legal assistance and, with the social worker's input, a parenting time agreement was reached.

Joint Custody Counseling

Mother and father had been married for only a year when the baby came. Shortly after the birth of the baby, the parents became emotionally detached from each other. However, both parents remained quite attached to the child. They mutually agreed to divorce, provided they could have joint custody with equal time. Each parent hired a lawyer, but they could not agree on the language of a custody agreement. The lawyers agreed to have their clients meet with a social worker to work out the details. The social worker devised an age-appropriate time-sharing system, and both parents agreed to honor it.[10]

SCOPE OF LAWYER'S INVOLVEMENT

When a client comes to see a lawyer during this stage, the lawyer's involvement depends on where the parties are in the time frame, as defined earlier. In the early stage of marital discord, often one spouse goes to a lawyer without advising the other spouse. The involvement of the lawyer at this stage is to answer questions regarding legal rights and to offer advice on how to protect these rights. If there is any desire to salvage the marriage, a referral to a mental health professional might be appropriate. A family lawyer should be aware of social workers in his or her community and what specific expertise they can provide.

---

[10]This exemplifies a common point in textbooks on family therapy that advise: "Clearly defined rules and responsibilities are essential [after divorce] for the sake of the children. When coparenting problems arise, therapy may be of great value." David L. Fenell and Barry K. Weinhold, *Counseling Families: An Introduction to Marriage and Family Therapy*, 2nd edition, page 306 (Denver: Love Publishing Co., 1997).

If the social worker is able to work with both spouses and the children, then that social worker might be in a good position to recommend a specific custody arrangement that would best advantage the parties' children. If both spouses have developed a good rapport with and respect for the social worker, then the possibility that they might reach an agreeable custody arrangement would be greatly enhanced. The lawyer could take the agreed-upon custody recommendations of the social worker and incorporate them into a separation agreement. Although an agreement prepared by the lawyer with input from the social worker in most cases would ensure effectiveness and fairness, situations can arise that require adjustments to avoid court intervention. A provision in the separation agreement whereby the social worker would monitor the custody arrangement (although of questionable enforceability) might help the arrangement work more effectively.

SCOPE OF SOCIAL WORKER'S INVOLVEMENT

A social worker who has a cognitive understanding of the dynamics of family life and has developed techniques for dealing with intrapersonal and familial problems should be able to readily extend his or her knowledge and techniques into the area of child custody. Such a social worker could be extremely helpful to families and to courts.

There are already a number of social workers serving as custody counselors all across the country. Many are disenchanted with the traditional custody trial, in which parents face each other in court like "gladiators in battle" (analogy developed by Woody, 1978, p. 57). They prefer to use their knowledge and skills helping parents and children maintain positive feelings for each other during the stressful period of separation or divorce.

Social workers can play an important role in the marital discord stage. When they team up with family lawyers to design custody agreements, they bring to the team a background in child growth and development and counseling techniques—subjects not taught in law school. As lawyers may be skilled at negotiating with adults, social workers may be skilled at identifying the needs of children. As lawyers often see a signed custody agreement as the end of the case, social workers often see it as a new beginning for family members.

One area in which social workers have made a significant difference is joint custody. The phrase "frequent and continued contact with both parents" was developed by the Joint Custody Association,[11] a national organization based in California social workers, behavioral scientists, and other mental health professionals. The concept of joint custody derives its cognitive base from the field of child development, and it has achieved remarkable statu-

---

[11] 10606 Wilkins Avenue, Los Angeles, CA 90024; phone: 310-475-5352.

tory[12] momentum across the United States. When the social worker hears the "child's best interests," it sounds like a familiar term from his or her own discipline. A child is nurtured by caring adults, so the social worker is concerned about the family's best interests.

PRACTICAL TECHNIQUES

Questions

Some intake questions the social worker might ask during the interview sessions with parents are as follows:

- What is the problem; how can I help you?
- One at a time, can you tell me what you consider are the major problems in your home life now?
- What positive features can be found today in your home life? In other words, what are the points of strength, if any, in your family life at the present time?
- How are these issues at home affecting the children?
- Have you discussed the marital discord problem with the children? How did each child respond?
- Can each of you describe any special needs of the children at this time (relationship with siblings; mental and physical health; special relationship with relatives, friends at school, and so forth)? Do the children participate in any religious activities? Which parent has been more involved in the child's religious activities?
- Can each of you give an example that epitomizes your discipline system?
- Who has been the primary caretaker[13] of the child or children during the previous six months?

---

[12]In 1979, the first joint custody statute was enacted in California (Family Code, section 4600) followed in 1987 by Kansas (Kan. Stat. Ann. § 60-1610) and Oregon (Or. Rev. Stat. § 107.169). By 2008, 44 states and the District of Columbia had enacted statutes that specifically authorize trial court judges to order joint, or shared, legal custody. Of these 44 states, 14 states declared some sort of presumption in favor of joint custody. This means that courts are supposed to grant joint custody unless there is proof that joint custody is not in the child's best interest. Six states do not have joint custody statutes, but courts in these states can use their equitable powers to order joint custody in appropriate circumstances. When social workers conduct custody evaluations, they should be aware of the legal status of joint custody in the states where they conduct evaluations.

[13]There is a large body of case law that places significant weight on the primary caretaker doctrine. It became a presumptive custody factor in West Virginia (*Garska v. McCoy*, 278 S.E.2d 357 (1981)), but other states responded differently. For example, it was introduced the following year in Pennsylvania (*Jordan v. Jordan*, 302 Pa. Super. 421, 448 A.2d 1113 (1982)), but it was not presumptive. In some states, the doctrine was codified as a statutory custody factor: Ariz. Rev. Stat. § 25-403 A-7 (2003); Ky. Rev. Stat. § 405.020 (2003); and Tenn. Code § 36-6-106 (a)(2) (2003).

- Who has been the primary decision maker in the family during the past six months (planning family events, scheduling events for children, and so forth)?
- What parenting times are devoted to the children by each of you now?
- Have you discussed future living arrangements if you separate? What are the arrangements for parenting time with the children?
- If you have school-age children, have either of you noticed any changes in their attitudes or grades?
- How do you feel about coming back for another session to discuss in more detail the matters that have been raised today?

Follow-Up Materials

Depending on what discussions came out of the interview sessions, the social worker might want to invite the parents to read materials related to their interests (see Stage 1—Marital Discord in the Bibliography).

Plans in general. Some common yearly parenting plans appropriate for initial custody are the following:

- *Alternate weeks.* The children will be with the mother and father on alternate weeks. The children will transfer between mother's and father's custody at 6:00 P.M. Sundays.
- *Alternate months.* The children will be with the mother and father on alternate months. The children will transfer between mother's and father's custody at 6:00 P.M. the first Sunday of the month.
- *Split weeks and alternating weekends for school-age children.* The children will be with their mother from Mondays until after school on Wednesdays; the children will be with their father from after school on Wednesdays until after school on Fridays. The children will spend alternate weekends with each parent. Weekends will commence after school on Fridays and conclude at the beginning of school on Mondays.
- *Alternate weekends and midweek night.* The children will be with each parent on alternate weekends from 5:00 P.M. Friday until 9:00 A.M. Monday and from Wednesday evening at 6:00 P.M. until 9:00 A.M. Thursday on those Wednesdays not followed by that parent's weekend. The children will be with the other parent at all other times.

Plans for holidays. Some common plans for sharing holidays are as follows:

- *Alternate major holidays.* The children will be with their mother during the Christmas holidays in the (odd or even) years and with their father in the (even or odd) years. Similar recommendations might be made for Thanksgiving and the spring recess from school.

- *Split major holidays.* The children will be with one parent until halfway through the holiday and then transfer to the other parent.
- *Specific one-day holidays.* The children will be with their mother on Mother's Day and with their father on Father's Day. Each parent will have parenting time during the child's birthday.

2

Initial Custody Stage

DEFINITION AND TIME FRAME

Initial custody means the first time legal custody has been assigned or awarded by a court. The assignment can be by agreement, if incorporated into a court order, or it can be the result of a court hearing. Initial custody can be sole or joint. Legal terms vary from state to state—for example, some other terms used for custody are "shared custody" in Pennsylvania, "parental responsibility" in Florida, and "managing conservatorship" in Texas.

The initial custody stage includes that period between the filing of the Complaint for custody and the court order that creates the custody order. This time period can be as little as a few days or as long as several years. Although the length of time is generally insignificant in terms of the record of proceedings, it is quite significant in terms of the emotional life of the litigants.

The problems between the parents may have been years in the making. Either or both parents may have considered filing for custody in the past, but neither has. Initial custody means the custody issue has entered the public arena for the first time.

SOCIAL WORK INTERVENTION

At the initial custody stage, the scope for social work intervention is greater than that at the marital discord stage. The opportunity for professional assistance is greater because the parents are in an adversarial relationship. *Adversary* means one who opposes or resists—the dictionary uses the term "enemy" as the synonym. This may be the first time the parents have been in a legal adversary relationship. They may be naïve about the entire custody situation. Each may be going around frantically eliciting friends to testify on his or her behalf. The spirit of cooperation once in their marriage may have turned into bitter competition. The "old time" marital friends may be cautious about what they say and may not want to get involved—feeling that testifying in court for one parent will damage the relationship with the other parent. A neighbor might find it difficult to testify against one parent who might continue to be a neighbor.

This is often the atmosphere during the initial custody stage. There is tremendous need to gather information about the parents and the child. The information each parent has about the other decreases as the avenues of exchange of information become narrower. The parents know less and less about day-to-day events in the lives of the other. They do not speak much to each other because they have hired attorneys to speak for them.

Their attorneys have told both parents that the preferred way of communicating with each other is through them. Letters between the two attorneys are beginning to thicken the file. Even the most rudimentary topics of discourse are communicated through the attorneys' letters. The situation can be quite frustrating to that parent who may prefer to communicate directly with the other parent. The frustration intensifies in that parent who does not yet grasp the full meaning of being on the other side of a lawsuit against the very person with whom love recently was shared. Anxieties often run high at this initial stage of custody litigation. A parent may ask: How can my attorney meaningfully communicate for me without knowing the person I have been married to for all those years? The rift between the parents often increases by correspondence between their respective attorneys. Consider the following:

Dear Attorney Two,

I have recently spoken with my client about your client's desire to visit Bobby over the weekend of the third instead of the regularly scheduled weekend, which is the 10th.

My client feels that your client can find some other time to take Bobby on the fishing trip. Furthermore, my client has already made plans for Bobby for the weekend of the third.

Sincerely yours,

Attorney One
cc: Client

Dear Attorney One,

I have received your letter regarding our request for Bobby to be allowed to go on the fishing trip. My client feels that this may be the only time this summer that Bobby will have to see his cousin Tony who is visiting from Canada.

My client believes that Bobby should be the one to decide about things like fishing. I tend to agree with this. I understand his cousin Tony spent last summer with Bobby and they got to be very close.

I hope that your client doesn't continue to keep Bobby apart from his family members on this side of his family. That would be unfortunate.

Very truly yours,

Attorney Two
cc: Client

The rift between the parents can easily create suspicion and mistrust. Each parent feels that his or her every behavior is being watched by the other parent. Television programs are reminders that private detectives are often used in custody cases. Sometimes parents will rent safety deposit boxes at the bank to hide incriminating letters from sweethearts. Some will rent post office boxes for fear that their mail may be opened. The tensions and hostilities at the initial custody stage often change the parents' personalities and habits.

The children see what is happening but do not understand it. They know that Mommy and Daddy are acting differently from the way they used to. Their contact with their parents and grandparents becomes strained, and they sometimes act out their feelings at home and at school. When their emotional damage becomes visible, each parent blames the other for the children's depression or aggressiveness.

Furthermore, the parents are sometimes so busy with their own emotions concerning the marital separation that time for the children becomes a low priority. The scope of social work intervention at the initial custody stage is described in the literature in several disciplines. Professional journals in the fields of psychology, divorce counseling, social work, family therapy, orthopsychiatry, and child welfare are filled with articles related to child custody. Research has described the child custody contest as one of the major emotional crises in an individual's life.

The more intense the adversarial relationship is between the parents, the greater the need is for social work intervention. The social worker can be of tremendous assistance in keeping a parent from going off the deep end. The parent experiencing single parenthood for the first time may be overwhelmed by the task. The parent experiencing separation from the child may feel emotionally isolated. Having someone to talk to during this period of time should not be underestimated. In short, there is often great need for professional involvement during the initial custody stage.

This is the first stage where a custody evaluator may be agreed upon or appointed by the court. The order of appointment typically states that the parties are to cooperate with the evaluator, sign the appropriate releases for confidential information, and make the child available to the evaluator at his or her request.

The evaluator then proceeds to interview the parties and, possibly, the child; observe the parenting skills in each home; interview lay and professional collaterals; conduct home studies; sometimes administer personality tests; and organize the data in terms of the custody factors from statute or case law. The evaluator then presents recommendations in a comprehensive custody report sent to both parties and the court.

CASE EXAMPLES

Not all initial custody cases require the involvement of a social worker or a lawyer. If a lawyer is retained, he or she should carefully assess the nature of the case to determine whether a social worker will be of value. Although each case is unique in some respects, most cases will fall into general categories. The following case examples, of course, are not exhaustive of all initial custody situations. The intention is to demonstrate the diversity of family life situations. The following examples are grouped by whether a social worker is needed.

Social Worker Not Needed

- *Settlement is pending.* The attorneys have had several conferences, and they have narrowed down the issues relating to the children. Neither side has indicated that the children are having difficulty, and the pending settlement promises to provide both parents with reasonable periods of time with the children.
- *Older child with clear preference.* Mother and father have been residing apart for a year. Mother works as a flight attendant for a national airline and is often away from her apartment for several days at a time. Father is an automobile mechanic with his shop in the barn adjacent to the marital home where he continues to reside with his son. The boy is 16 years old and a senior in high school. He has a part-time job and works with his father on weekends. The boy loves his mother, but states a clear preference to remain with his father. The attorney has interviewed potential witnesses, including the neighbors, the boy's minister, and the high school coach, all of whom describe a well-adjusted and emotionally mature boy.
- *Long-term physical possession.* An unwed Connecticut mother left her six-year-old daughter with her parents and moved to California. Six months ago, she was involuntarily admitted to a psychiatric ward and refuses to relinquish custody. She has a long history of mental disorders and a lengthy police report. The father is unknown—the maternal grandparents have raised the little girl since birth. The child has always resided in the grandparents' home, which is a section of town known to be a good neighborhood.

Social Worker Needed

- *Both parents fit and proper.* The marriage was 16 years; both parents work full-time and are equally involved with the children: a boy age 11 and a girl age 13. Each parent is thoroughly convinced of his or her position regarding the children's needs, and each parent believes the children's best interests should be paramount. Neither parent has any "ugliness" on record.
- *Allegation that child fears parent.* The Complaint for custody contains the allegation that the five-year-old child fears one parent, but the parent being accused calls it a lie. That parent is distraught that some minor events in the couple's past are now blown out of proportion. It is a matter of one parent's word against the other.
- *Split siblings.* One parent feels the children should remain together and the other parent feels the siblings should be divided in the custody agreement. The children are of different sexes, and they are ages nine and 11 years. All four grandparents reside in the same area as the couple, and each set of grandparents is siding along family lines. The parents have different reasons to support their respective viewpoints, but both are concerned about the children's future and want what is best for them.
- *Joint custody.* Mother and father have been married for nine years and have two children: a boy age 8 and a girl age 6. Mother filed for divorce and asked for sole custody, but the father wants joint custody because he has been regularly involved with most of the child-rearing duties. When the attorneys met and discussed joint custody, it became apparent that they each had different views. Neither parent claims the other is unfit, and both recognize that the other has demonstrated good parenting qualities over the years.
- *Expert on one side.* One parent was served with a Complaint for custody with an attached report from a psychologist recommending sole custody— the psychologist has never seen this parent.
- *False allegation of sexual abuse.* One parent was served with a Complaint for custody that contains allegations of sexual misconduct with the couple's three-year-old child. The accused parent knows this is untrue and initially laughs it off. But after talking to a lawyer about the possible ramifications, this parent now believes that his or her relationship with the child is in serious jeopardy.

SCOPE OF LAWYER'S INVOLVEMENT

If the client is the plaintiff, the lawyer must prepare the Complaint for custody and have it served on the defendant. The lawyer initially obtains the factual base of the case from the client. The intake session or sessions with the client should be thorough enough to draft an effective Complaint, with enough detail on which to base a prayer for custody, yet with caution not to present a "blueprint" for the other side to counter or correct by the time of trial. When the Complaint focuses on the emotional health of the child, consultation with the child's psychologist before preparation of the Complaint may be of great value. Attaching a report from the psychologist might be persuasive. If circumstances are appropriate, a temporary custody order should be sought, along with a request for a custody evaluation that proposes the name of a social worker.

If the client is the defendant, the lawyer's intake session should include a thorough review of the Complaint with the client. The lawyer may want to employ the services of a social worker or other mental health professional to critique the report attached to the Complaint. The lawyer should select a professional whose experience and training are relevant to the factual base of the case. If a local professional is not available, the lawyer may obtain a referral from an appropriate national association (see Appendix C for a list of the mental health associations). Also, many county courts maintain a list of local mental health professionals qualified, and willing, to conduct child custody evaluations.

If a lawyer intends to use a social worker on one side of the case, a conference should be arranged to develop a case strategy. (Sometimes it is beneficial for the client to be present; sometimes not.) It may be a good idea to develop a theme for the case, and the social worker's input in designing the theme can be invaluable. For one thing, a theme can give the initial custody case some direction and make its presentation at trial cohesive. For another thing, a theme can provide the continuity between the lay testimony and the opinions advanced by the expert's testimony. With a theme developed between the lawyer and the social worker, the lawyer can select the various custody factors[14] to emphasize at trial, and select the order of the witnesses in terms of developing the theme for the court. Furthermore, the theme of the initial custody case may be child centered and have a theoretical base that can be expressed in the social worker's report and, if necessary, articulated at trial.

Some states have elevated to statutory importance the value of a recommendation from the custody evaluator. The Georgia state code in 2008 stated,

> in determining the best interests of the child, the judge may consider any relevant factor including . . . any recommendation by a court appointed custody evaluator or guardian ad litem. (§ 19-9-3 (3)(O))

---

[14]Some states have statutory custody factors; other states do not. All states, with or without statutory custody factors rely upon the best interests of the child principle. In some states, best interest is defined by statutory custody factors. For example, custody factors are found in Del. Code Ann. § 13-722 (2005); Fla. Stat. § 61.13 (3) (2008); Mich. Comp. Laws § 722.23 (2008); Mont. Code Ann. § 40-4-212 (2007); N.J. Stat. Ann. § 9:2-4 (2008); Or. Rev. Stat. § 107.137 (2008); and Va. Code § 20-124.3 (2008). Examples of states without statutory custody factors are N.C. Gen. Stat. § 50-13.2 (2008) and 23 Pa. Cons. Stat. Ann. § 101 (2008).

SCOPE OF SOCIAL WORKER'S INVOLVEMENT

In an initial custody case, if one of the attorneys contacts a social worker, he or she may be reluctant to become involved for fear of being labeled a "hired gun" and, therefore, may insist on having access to both parents as well as the children. Sometimes the attorney can approach the other side and obtain a stipulation that both parents cooperate with the social worker. If an attempted stipulation is unsuccessful, one attorney may motion the court for an order directing both parents to cooperate with the social worker.

If the social worker is working only with one side of the case, a partnership may develop between the social worker and the attorney. As long as the partnership directs itself toward the child's best interests, there is nothing improper or unprofessional. This partnership can sometimes develop a fuller understanding of the psychosocial dimensions of the case, which may otherwise go lacking.

It is important, however, that the custody evaluator who has had access to only one side of the case is not in a strong position to offer a custody recommendation to the court. The American Academy of Psychiatry and the Law (2005) has recognized this in *Ethics Guidelines for the Practice of Forensic Psychiatry.* According to Guideline IV, it may be inappropriate to comment on the fitness of a parent whom you have not interviewed.

Regardless of which side hires the social worker to conduct a custody evaluation, the best interests of the child always predominate. In other words, the evaluator must not be an advocate for the side that pays the fee for fear of the accusation of developing opinions favoring that side of the case. Knowledgeable family court judges call this "confirmatory bias." According to Dalton, Drozd, and Wong (2006),

> One common flaw in reports prepared by custody evaluators that deserves special mention is "confirmatory bias." It appears when the evaluator develops a hypothesis—forms an opinion about some issue in the case—early in his or her process, finds data to support it, confirms the hypothesis, and then stops testing it against new or different data that might undermine the hypothesis or effect a change of mind. (p. 20)

The custody evaluator can guard against the accusation of bias by identifying data that are both favorable and unfavorable to the one side of the case evaluated and by identifying areas from which data were unobtainable.

The one-sided evaluation can measure the child's relationship with one parent and compare it with other parent–child relationships of similar age and gender. The social worker can also measure the child individually, in terms of the child's social–emotional–educational maturity. These various measures may suggest one type of mental health professional over another, depending on the particular factors involved in the case.

To measure the child's educational achievement and socialization into his or her school, a school guidance counselor may be appropriate. To measure the child's school performance, personal interviews with teachers and other school personnel might provide additional data to consider along with the academic grades. For younger children, if the school does not provide grading, a review of the "teacher's comments" section on the report card might prove helpful.

To measure the parent's ability to perform basic nurturing tasks and the ability to comprehend the needs of the child, a parent competency study might be conducted by a social worker, family counselor, psychologist, educator, or any other mental health professional.

For measuring the child's social–intellectual ability, the Wechsler Intelligence Scale for Children or the Thematic Apperception Test might be appropriate. The latter is purely subjective; the former is not. Used together, they might prove useful in some cases. Most mental health professionals can be authorized by the tests' publishers to administer them.

When joint custody is considered for initial custody, the social worker is extremely important. Joint custody is more acceptable today than it was in the past; but it continues to be held in disfavor by some. A classic, but negative, description from Texas Justice Alexander in *Martin v. Martin* (1939) read as follows:

> Certainly, no child could grow up normally when it is hawked about from one parent to the other with the embarrassing scene of changing homes at least twice each year. Such decrees are usually prompted by a laudable desire to avoid injuring the feelings of the parents, but the net result is a permanent injury to the child without any substantial benefit to the parents. In addition to the lack of stability in his surroundings, the child is constantly reminded that he is the center of a parental quarrel. It is readily apparent that such practices are calculated to arouse serious emotional conflicts in the mind of the child and are not conducive to good citizenship. Moreover, the parents are continuously pitted against each other in the unenviable contest of undermining the child's love for the other parent. Each parent is afraid to exercise any sort of discipline for fear of losing out in the contest. As a result, the child is reared without parental control. Such decrees by which the child is awarded part-time to each of the parents have been condemned by numerous decisions. (132 S.W.2d at 428)

In 1995, the Texas legislature amended the family code to allow joint custody, now called joint managing conservatorship. One parent may oppose joint custody because he or she believes the child cannot handle it. A thorough assessment of the child might place the social worker in a position of either recommending joint custody or sole custody.

The social worker conducting a custody evaluation should know the legal status of joint custody in the state having jurisdiction. In a few states, joint custody is presumed to be best for the child, but this presumption can be overcome by evidence to the contrary. In most states, however, there are statutory provisions for joint custody, and sometimes there are statutory factors that must be addressed to determine the suitability of such an arrangement. Thirty states[15] can order joint custody, but do not require it. Fourteen states and the District of Columbia[16] have some form of presumption in favor of joint custody. Six states[17] have no statute for joint custody, but courts can order it under their general equitable powers.

Custody evaluators understand that joint custody has two aspects: legal custody and physical custody. Physical custody (in some states called "parenting time") involves the actual time the child spends with each parent. Legal custody involves decisional authority over the child. Under joint legal custody, major decisions[18] regarding the child's health, education, religion, and welfare are to be shared between the parents. The idea that a court should order divorced or separated parents to have joint legal custody is an idea that has been questioned by many, including family court judges. However, a New York family court judge has recently suggested, "If we stopped thinking about 'joint legal custody' and instead thought about 'joint decision making' parents would be much better off."

---

[15]Ala. Code § 30-3-152(a) (1998); Alaska Stat. § 25.20.060 (Michie 2002); Ariz. Rev. Stat. Ann. § 25-403(B) (West Supp. 2003); Ark. Code Ann. § 9-13-101(B)(1)(A) (Michie Supp. 2003); Colo. Rev. Stat. Ann. § 14- 10-124(b) (West 1996); Del. Code Ann. tit. 13 §§ 722 & 727 (1999); Ga. Code Ann. § 19-9-6 (1) (1995); Haw. Rev. Stat. § 571-46.1 (1993); 750 Ill. Comp. Stat. Ann. 5/602.1(b) (West 1993); Ind. Code Ann. § 31-17-2-13 (Michie 2003); Ky. Rev. Stat. Ann. § 403.270 (Michie 2003); Md. Code Ann., Fam. Law § 5-203(d) (Supp. 2004); Mass. Gen. Laws Ann. ch. 208, § 31 (West Supp. 2004); Mich. Comp. Laws Ann. § 722.26a (West 2002); Mo. Ann. Stat. § 452.375 (West 2002); Neb. Rev. Stat. § 42-364(5) (Supp. 2004); N.J. Stat. Ann. § 9:2-4 (West 2002); N.C. Gen. Stat. § 50-13.2 (2003); Ohio Rev. Code Ann. § 3109.04(2) (West Supp. 2004); Okla. Stat. Ann. tit. 43, § 109(B) (West 2001); Or. Rev. Stat. § 107.105 (2003); 23 Pa. Cons. Stat. Ann. § 5304 (West 2001); S.D. Codified Laws § 25-5-7.1 (Michie 1999); Tenn. Code Ann. § 36-6-101(a)(1) (Supp. 2003); Tex. Fam. Code § 101.016 (1995); Utah Code Ann. § 30-3-10.2 (Supp. 2004); Va. Code Ann. § 20-124.2(B) (Michie 2004); Vt. Stat. Ann. tit. 15 § 665(a) (2002); W.Va. Code Ann. § 48-9-207(a) (Michie 2001); Wyo. Stat. Ann. § 20-2-201 (Michie 2003).

[16]Cal. Fam. Code § 3080 (West 1994); Conn. Gen. Stat. Ann. § 46b-56a (West 2003); D.C. Code Ann. § 16-914(a)(2) (Supp. 2004); Fla. Stat. Ann. § 61.13(2)(b) (2004); Idaho Code § 32-717B(4) (1996); Iowa Code Ann. § 598.41 (West 2000); Kan. Stat. Ann. § 60-1610(a)(4) (1994); La. Rev. Stat. Ann. § 9:335 (West 1999); Me. Rev. Stat. Ann. tit. 19-A § 1653(2) (West Supp. 2003); Minn. Stat. Ann. § 518.17(2) (West Supp. 2004); Miss. Code Ann. § 93-5-24(4) (Supp. 2003); Nev. Rev. Stat. Ann. § 125.490 (Michie 2004); N.H. Rev. Stat. Ann. § 458.17 (Supp. 2003); N.M. Stat. Ann. § 40-4-9.1 (Michie 1999); Wis. Stat. Ann. § 767.24 (2) (West Supp. 2003).

[17]Mont. Code Ann. § 40-4-212 (2003); N.Y. Dom. Rel. Law § 240 (McKinney Supp. 2004); N.D. Cent. Code § 14-09-06 (2003); R.I. Gen. Laws § 15-5-16 (2003); S.C. Code Ann. § 20-3-160 (Law. Co-op. 1984); Wash. Rev. Code Ann. § 26.09.002 (West 1996).

[18]Under Wisconsin statutes, for example, major decisions "include, but are not limited to, decisions regarding consent to marry, consent to enter military service, consent to obtain a motor vehicle operator's license, authorization for nonemergency health care and choice of school and religion" (Wis. Stat. § 767.001(2m) (2008).

The Hon. W. Dennis Duggan, F.C.J. in The Albany Court Bar Association Newsletter, April 2009, pp. 1–2, at page 1.

Some states provide for the distribution of decisional authority,[19] whereby one parent may be awarded sole legal decisional authority regarding, for example, the education of the child, whereas decisions regarding the child's health and religion must be shared. This provision can be tricky for the custody evaluator. For example, if the mother is a doctor, there may be an assumption that medical decisions must be vested solely in her; if the father is a teacher, the assumption may be that educational decisions must be vested solely in him. If the custody evaluator recommends distributing decisional authority, there should be sufficient data to conclude such unilateral decisional authority is warranted. Reasons should be carefully spelled out in the evaluator's report. Whether the social worker conducts a custody evaluation in a state that allows the distribution of decisional authority or not, it is important to consider the parents' history of sharing decisions and their propensity to do so in the future.

PRACTICAL TECHNIQUES

Sample direct examination questions to ask to qualify a social worker to offer expert testimony in court are as follows:

- Where are you employed and for how long?
- What is your position or job title?
- Can you briefly describe your professional employment history?
- What is your educational background?
- Do you have any other educational background (for example, continuing education courses, seminars, and so forth)?
- What, if anything, have you published in the field of social work?
- Have you presented any seminars, given any speeches, or taught any courses on a specific topic (name topic)?
- Have you had occasion to observe the children? For how long?
- Have you prepared a written report in connection with your professional services in this case?
- Do you have any opinions you believe would be of assistance to this court?

At this point, the lawyer should tender the witness to the court as an expert able to offer opinions about the child's best interests.

---

[19]For example, Wisconsin defines joint legal custody as "the condition under which both parties share legal custody and neither party's legal custody rights are superior, except with respect to specified decisions as set forth by the court or the parties in the final judgment or order" (Wis. Stat. § 767.001(1s) (2008)). See also Ala. Code § 30-3-151 (2) (1998); Ga. Code Ann. § 19-9-6 (2) (2008); and Tex. Fam. Code § 101.016 (2008).

Prior to trial the lawyer will need from the social worker (in addition to a current resume),

- definitions of technical terms that can be used at trial
- copies of any reports prepared
- other sources of information from which the social worker's opinions may be drawn, other than those reflected in his or her report
- any weaknesses the social worker found in the client not covered in the report
- extent of the social worker's knowledge with respect to the nature of the litigation
- impressions the social worker has of the child and how those impressions were obtained (the child's test results or anything the child might have said to the social worker)
- materials read by the social worker during the course of his or her study of the child
- social worker's knowledge of any of the parties socially prior to the beginning of his or her involvement in this case
- social worker's theme (bonding, sibling rivalry, reactive dependency, authority complex, and so forth, enabling the lawyer to integrate all the facets of the case around this central theme.

The social worker will need from the lawyer

- description of court procedures
- positioning in the courtroom
- materials to bring to court (reports, files, charts, and so forth) and video or audio equipment needed to augment the testimony
- expectation of cross-examination from opposing lawyer
- time required at the trial
- style and order of his or her testimony at trial
- do's and don'ts for social worker when testifying—*do* be prompt, dress appropriately, relax, be clear and concise, and be organized and professional; *don't* ramble, speak in monologue, speak too fast, be redundant, be argumentative on cross-examination, and answer confusing or misunderstood questions).

Personality Tests

In addition, personality tests often are used in initial custody cases. Licensing boards and most of the publishers of these tests usually authorize their use.[20]

---

[20]Many custody evaluators have a clinical practice. Clinicians should understand there is a major difference between testing and clinically interviewing "parents" versus "custody litigants." Patients often come voluntarily for treatment, but custody litigants usually come reluctantly with one primary question: How do I best present myself to "win" custody?

Minnesota Multiphasic Personality Inventory (MMPI). The original MMPI was developed from interviews and multiple-choice questions given to mental patients in a rural Scandinavian area of Minnesota in the 1930s and 1940s. Later, several University of Minnesota psychology professors developed a questionnaire of over 500 items to assist clinicians in diagnosing mental illnesses, such as depression, schizophrenia, and hypochondrias. From their responses, the developers created 13 scales, 10 of which measured personality whereas the other three scales measured the validity of the test itself. Some MMPI tests are abbreviated forms with anywhere from 71 to 168 questions.

A second version, the MMPI-2, was first published in 1989. Over the years, the MMPI-2 has been updated, but there has yet to be an edition aimed specifically at assessing personality for parenting. The MMPI-2 is an instrument that can offer insight into personality traits that can be helpful to evaluators when integrated with other procedures, such as observations.

Bender Visual Motor Gestalt Test (Bender). This test, designed in 1938, is primarily used for diagnosing brain damage, but can also be used to detect emotional problems. Nine black geometric designs are shown sequentially to the subject who is asked to reproduce them on paper. The test takes anywhere from three to 15 minutes, and is subjectively interpreted by the examiner. Maturity in young children and emotional disturbance in older children and adults can sometimes be indicated by this test.

Thematic Apperception Test (TAT). A Harvard University professor developed the TAT in 1938. There are 20 pictures of people in a variety of situations. Any number of the 20 pictures can be shown to the subject. Then the subject is asked to make up a story about each picture. The stories told usually reveal information about the subject's emotional conflicts. The children's version, called the Children's Apperception Test (CAT), has 10 pictures and portrays animals in various situations instead of people.

Projective drawings. The subject is asked to draw a picture of a person, house, family, and so forth. The idea is that the subject will project himself or herself and family members into the drawings. Mental health professionals have attempted to standardize the interpretations of the drawings, but they have been unsuccessful. This test may be especially useful for young children, although it is often used as a secondary test rather than a primary one because it is so individualistic.

Millon Clinical Multiaxial Inventory (MCMI-III). Developed in 1954 by Professor Theodore Millon, who taught abnormal psychology at Lehigh University, in Allentown, Pennsylvania, the MCMI-III is a 25-minute, 175-item true–false self-reporting test. Professor Millon and his students went on tours of Allentown State Hospital, and he went alone on numerous visits. "These visits became, in effect, the motivation and substantive foundation [for my] career that ultimately lead to the development of new diagnostic tools (e.g., MCMI)" (http://www.millon.net/content/tm_bio.htm).

This test's norms were created from 998 men and women with a variety of diagnoses. The population included patients from clinics, private practices, mental health centers, residential settings, and hospitals. The instrument is used to "identify personality characteristics underlying a patient's present symptoms" (http://www.pearsonassessments.com/mcmi.aspx).

Personality Assessment Inventory (PAI). First introduced in 1991, the PAI has 344 items and takes less than an hour to complete. Test takers are allowed four gradations of response ("false," "slightly true," "mainly true," and "very true") rather than being forced to respond only "true" or "false," and the items are comprehensible at the fourth-grade reading level. This test is an objective inventory of adult personality that assesses psychopathological syndromes.

Parenting Stress Index (PSI). The PSI test consists of 120 items and takes less than 30 minutes for the parent to complete. It is designed for the early identification of parenting and family characteristics that fail to promote normal development and functioning in children, children with behavioral and emotional problems, and parents who are at risk of dysfunctional parenting. The PSI identifies dysfunctional parenting and predicts the potential for parental behavior problems. Although its primary focus is on the preschool child, the PSI can be used with parents whose children are 12 years old or younger.

Rubric—Similarity in Testing

Custody evaluators should be aware of the principle of "substantial similarity of conditions,"[21] when administering tests to the parents. This principle does not require absolute identity; however, the tests must "be so nearly the same in substantial particulars as to afford a fair comparison in respect to the particular issue to which the test is directed." [Footnote: *Illinois Central Gulf R.R. v Ishee*, 317 So.2d 923 at 926 (Miss. 1975). See also *Jackson v. Fletcher*, 647 F.2d 1020 (10th Cir. 1981).]

This principle is important for custody evaluators who may be called to testify as an expert. If the tests are different, or if the testing conditions are different, then there would be no fair basis for comparing the respective test results. The principle has been stated this way: When an expert bases an opinion on a series of tests, the circumstance and conditions for each test must be similar."[22]

---

[21]The substantial similarity principle is premised on the judicial belief that dissimilarity of the conditions under which tests were administered could distort the evidentiary value of evidence. More than 100 years ago, the Florida Supreme Court stated, "in many instances, a slight change in the conditions under which the experiment is made will so distort the result as to wholly destroy its value as evidence, and make it harmful, rather than helpful" (*Hisler v. State*, 42 So. 692, 695[Fla. 1906]).

[22]Husky Industries, Inc. v. Black, 434 So.2d 988; 993, Fla. 4th DCA 1983.

Caution about Psychological Testing

Psychological tests, although frequently administered by clinicians, are not always received well by courts. As one chief judge in Florida in *Keesee v. Keesee* (1996) commented on her concern about their use:

> I am increasingly concerned about the proliferating and extensive use of psychologists in these family law cases and the extreme reliance trial courts appear to place on their opinions. These experts have been allowed to offer opinions on . . . who is telling the truth and who is "in denial.". . . These psychological evaluations in many cases amount to no more than an exercise in human lie detection. . . . After several years of reading reports in these cases, my own confidence in such evidence has fallen very low. (675 So.2d at 660)

Custody-Specific Tests

In addition, four tests specifically for assessing a parent's knowledge and ability are useful in child custody evaluations.

Parent Competency Study (PCS). The PCS is an assessment of a parent's ability to be successful in a single-parent environment. The four parts of the study are (1) make several direct observations of each parent's interactions with the child in diverse situations (this will be useful to compare parenting skills); (2) measure the parent's level of knowledge of parenting skills by asking a series of questions relevant to the age of the child being evaluated; (3) evaluate and compare the parent–child interactions in terms of trust, affection, and behavioral competency for responding to the needs of the child; and (4) measure each parent's general knowledge of home management.

The PCS requires two skills from the evaluator. Observation skills are used to compare parent–child interactions, and interview skills are used to assess the parents' knowledge about child growth and development. The PCS can be an effective instrument for the evaluator to obtain direct information from the parents about their parenting knowledge and to integrate that information into the parents' child-rearing abilities. Direct observation (and opinions derived therefrom) can provide valuable testimony should the case go to trial.

Bricklin Perceptual Scales (BPS). The BPS scales, developed in the 1980s, are used primarily for child custody evaluations. The BPS's Parent Perception of Child Profile Scale attempts to measure a parent's knowledge of the child's social milieu, communication style, daily routines, and basic fears. Questionnaires, including hypothetical questions, are presented to each parent, and their responses portray their comparative parenting styles.

The BPS attempts to measure and compare a child's perception of his or her parents in four different areas: competency, supportiveness, follow-up consistency, and possession of admirable qualities. The parent who receives the higher ratings on 32 questions is deemed the parent more likely to be able to serve the child's best interest.

Ackerman-Scoendorf Scales for Parent Evaluation of Custody (ASPECT). The ASPECT instrument was developed in 1992. It produces an overall score (the Parental Custody Index) that can guide custody recommendations. It attempts to tell which parent is more effective, and how much more effective one parent is than the other. If neither parent is effective, the PCI will reflect that too. In addition, ASPECT differentiates situations in which one parent should obtain full custody from those in which joint custody may be appropriate, and it may be effective in identifying parents who need supervision during visitations. The ASPECT requires the evaluator to answer yes-or-no questions based on information obtained from ASPECT and interviews with and observation of each parent with and without the child.

Perception of Relations Test (PORT). Developed in 1989, the PORT measures the degree to which a child seeks emotional closeness with each parent. It is made up of seven tasks, mostly drawings that measure the strengths and weaknesses between the child and each parent. Specifically, it measures the child's tendency to behave in certain ways (aggressively, assertively, fearfully, and so forth) toward each parent. It can provide insight into the child's perceptions of each parent and is often administered in conjunction with other appropriate instruments.

Questions for Social Worker's Initial Intake Session

The following suggested questions are divided into two parts—questions for the parents and questions for the children.

Questions for Parents

- Have you committed a felony?
- Have you been in jail or prison?
- Have you used illegal drugs?
- Have you abused prescription drugs? Alcohol?
- Have you been arrested for, or convicted of, driving while under the influence of alcohol or other drugs?
- Have you engaged in gambling activities? Any illegal activities?
- Have you attempted suicide?
- Have you been hospitalized for an emotional or psychiatric disorder?
- Have you suffered from, or received treatment for, an emotional or psychiatric condition?
- Have you abused your spouse? Your child?
- Have you had a sexual relationship during the marriage with someone other than your spouse?
- Have you had a sexual relationship with someone other than your spouse whom the children knew about?

- Have you had a homosexual relationship? Engaged in unusual sexual practices?
- Have you had a pregnancy outside of marriage?
- Have you had a venereal disease?
- Does your work require travel?
- Is your work schedule likely to change in the future?
- What are your plans for child care?
- What are your housing arrangements, including number of bedrooms?
- Do the children have any social or unusual educational or health care needs?
- Who has worked to meet those needs?
- Has the division of responsibility for child care changed over the years?
- What times do you spend with the children?
- Have the children's academic performance changed in the last few years or months?
- What are the children's grades?
- Have you ever interfered with your children's relationship with your spouse or undermined it in any way?
- Have you or your spouse blocked the other parent's access to the children?
- Have you or your spouse undermined the children's relationship with a significant other person or family member?
- How well have you been able to cooperate on matters concerning the children?
- How well have you and your spouse in the past been able to share decision making regarding the children?
- To what extent do you and your spouse share values regarding how children should be raised?
- Have you or your spouse moved in the last 10 years?
- Do you or your spouse plan to move in the near future?
- Who has been the child's primary caretaker?[23]
- Do the children have a particularly close relationship with any family member on your side of the family?
- What are your goals and reasons for your goals regarding child rearing?
- What are your spouse's goals regarding child rearing?
- Have you and your spouse attempted to negotiate a settlement between yourselves? If so, what progress did you make? What are your present positions?

---

[23]Some states include "primary caretaker" in their statutory custody factors and other states do not. For example, Minnesota and Oregon include the primary caretaker factor (Minn. Stat. § 518.17 subdivision 1 (a)(3) (2008); Or. Rev. Stat. § 107.137(1)(e) (2008)), but it is not included in Connecticut's statutory factors (see Conn. Gen. Stat. §§ 46b-56 (c)(1–16) (2008)).

Although the custody evaluator should be responsible for comprehensive inquiry into this topic in those states where primary caretaker is a statutory factor, the evaluator may find relevant data on this topic even in those states where it is not a statutory factor.

- Who has knowledge of your relationship and your spouse's relationship with the children and your ability and your spouse's ability to raise the children?

Questions for the Children

- Who prepares your meals?
- Who arranges for medical and dental care and takes you to doctors' appointments?
- Who shops for your clothes?
- Who takes you to extracurricular activities?
- What recreational or educational activities do your parents do with you?
- Do you receive religious training? If so, from whom?
- Who arranges your birthday parties?
- Who helps you with your homework?
- Who attends parent–teacher conferences?
- To whom do you turn when you have a problem?
- Who selects your babysitters? (Get names of the sitters for possible interviews.)
- How do you get along with your siblings?
- Who helps you get dressed in the morning?
- Who bathes and grooms you?
- Who gives you permission to get together with your friends?
- Who puts you to bed at night?
- Who cares for you when you are ill?
- Who disciplines you and by what method?

3

Visitation Denial Stage

DEFINITION AND TIME FRAME

Visitation is both the child's right and the noncustodial parent's right. Visitation implies the right for the child and the noncustodial parent to spend meaningful time together away from the custodial parent. These time periods can be long or short; they can be scheduled or flexible; and they derive from agreement or court order.[24]

The time frame for the denial of visitation stage is after the initial custody award has been entered and before it has been modified. Denial of visitation can begin immediately after the initial custody order has been entered in court, but attorneys usually tell their noncustodial clients to wait until more than one denial has occurred before bringing the matter to court. Therefore, although visitation may in fact be denied, the matter may not appear in court until a pattern of denial has been established or until an incident arises that the noncustodial parent feels is important.

---

[24]States differ in their language. For example, in Pennsylvania, the term "visitation" is defined as "the right to visit a child. The term does *not* include the right to remove a child from the custodial parent's control. . . . Partial custody [is defined as] the right to take possession of a child away from the custodial parent for a certain period of time" (23 Pa. Cons. Stat. § 5302 (2008)). In other states, the term "visitation" has been replaced with the term "parenting time."

SOCIAL WORK INTERVENTION

The scope of social work intervention at the visitation denial stage is often greater than at the initial custody stage. Here, the court has completed its work, a decision has been rendered, and a plan for the child's relationship with both parents has been formulated. Whatever legal and mental health professionals the parents might have had at the initial custody stage usually have been discharged from duty, and the parents find themselves back in their private worlds.

The lives of the parents and children are supposed to be more orderly now than during the period of litigation—orderly in the sense that a conclusion has been reached and a judgment has been rendered about their children's custody. The court order prescribes each parent's duties and responsibilities for the children.

The court has rendered its decision—a judgment based on evidence and devoid of passion—under the guiding principle of law. It was a child-centered decision and rational under the circumstances presented, and within the boundaries of the rules of procedure. The appeal period passes and neither parent asks a higher court to review the case. Now, everything is up to the parents themselves to abide by the dictates of the initial custody order.

The social worker will be quick to see that the above synopsis of the way it is supposed to be is rarely the way it is. The above synopsis fails to take account of the emotional expectations. Look what the system is asking of the parents!

> Hey, you two people, we know that both of you were once in love, and you shared the most intimate factors of your private thoughts and aspirations with each other. We know that together you made a lovely child and, at least in the beginning, you were each thrilled in your newly found parenthood. We know that together you didn't make the marriage work, and we don't really think that your child was to blame for that. We know that our legal system provided you with ample time and appropriate procedures to have your dispute over the child heard before an impartial trier of fact. You had your day in court, facing each other as adversaries, fighting for the right to raise your child, whom we believe you both love equally. Now that the trial is over and we have named one of you as the "winner" and the other as the "loser," we are expecting both of you to go to your separate homes and behave properly, according to the separate parenthood roles that we have assigned to you.

Considering this synopsis, what are the chances that both parents will live up to the court's expectations for harmony and order in the life of the child? The need for social work intervention lurks everywhere.

From the social work perspective, custody of the child implies a responsibility to provide the nurturing elements appropriate to the child's age and circumstances. According to the court, the child needs to maintain association with the noncustodial parent. It labeled that system of contact "visitation." Denial of visitation is denying the child's opportunity for parental association. Do all custodial parents know this? Apparently, many do not. Postdivorce litigation abounds because of this very problem. Social science research shows the child of divorce develops a sense of self-esteem in proportion to his or her continued association with the visitation parent: "The greater the contact [with the noncustodial parent], the higher the sense of self-esteem" (Clarwar, 1982, p. 14). One would think the custodial parent would bend over backwards to enhance the child's sense of self-esteem—for a well-developed child is a credit to the custodial parent.

The scope of social work intervention at this stage is enormous. Visitation is often denied under the most ingenious pretenses, but usually on the claim that the custodial parent is "protecting" the child. The role of the social worker at this stage calls for not only understanding the pretext for denial, but also measuring the effects of the denial on the child.[25]

CASE EXAMPLES

When visitation is denied for unavoidable reasons, or because of circumstances out of the custodial parent's control, social work intervention is generally unnecessary. However, when denial is spiteful or contrived under a phony pretext, professional intervention may be helpful.

The following case examples are divided into those in which the intervention of a social worker may not be needed and those in which such intervention may be needed.

Social Worker Not Needed

- *Misunderstanding between parents.* Mother has custody, and father has alternate weekend visitation. For three consecutive weekends, father arrived at mother's house, but no one was there. Father files for contempt, and the attorneys have a conference to discuss the problem. Mother's attorney expresses the client's sincere apology and states that the mother got the weekends mixed up. Compensatory time is offered to the father, and he accepts it.
- *Child is out of the country.* Father has sole custody, and mother has visitation during the Christmas holidays. Father receives a wire from Paris that his father is critically ill, notifies mother, and flies with his son to France

---

[25]The role of the social worker as evaluator here should not be confused with the role of the social worker as therapist. Stuart Greenberg and Daniel Shuman list 10 ways in which the role of the evaluator differs from that of the therapist. See their "Irreconcilable Conflict Between Therapeutic and Forensic Roles," *28, Professional Psychology: Research & Practice*, 50–57 (1997).

that night. While in France, the Christmas holidays begin, but the child becomes sick and remains with his father in Paris for two weeks. Mother files a contempt action in court. Father and son return at the end of the Christmas holidays. Son plans on seeing mother during Easter vacation, which is not her visitation period.

Social Worker Needed

- *Visitation not exercised over time.* Father has sole custody of two high school daughters, and mother has "reasonable" visitation, but has not exercised it in over four years. Father has remarried, and his daughters have emotionally bonded with their stepmother. Mother telephones father for permission to resume visits, and he passes the phone to the oldest daughter, who tells mother that she does not want to see her again. Mother files an action in court; it could be a petition for contempt or a petition for enforcement. The court may be asked to appoint a custody evaluator at this point.
- *Delayed denial.* Mother has sole custody of an eight-year-old son. Father's visitation has been sporadic over the past two years. He tried to see the boy on several occasions, but frequently was denied visits. He never brought action in court. Recently, when father came to visit, his son ran out the back door. Father brings an action in court alleging parental alienation. The court may appoint a custody evaluator to determine whether parental alienation has occurred.
- *Denial by fear.* Mother has joint custody of two girls, ages seven and nine years. The children have been "quiet" on recent visits with their father, and their mother begins denying further visits, saying the girls are afraid to go with him. Father believes mother is "poisoning" their minds, and mother believes something horrible must have happened to the daughters on a recent visit. Father files a petition to enforce visitation.
- *Denial for protection.* Father has joint legal custody and primary residence; mother has alternate weekend visitation. Father claims that mother's cohabiter has a police record and keeps an unregistered handgun in the house. Father denies visitation on grounds that he is protecting his child from danger. Mother files for contempt of court.
- *No pay no see.* Mother has joint legal custody with primary residency; father has visitation on the first and third weekends and every Wednesday night. Mother claims father's child support is two months late and tells him he can't exercise his visitation until he pays in full. Father files a petition for contempt and asks the court to appoint a custody evaluator to assist the court in determining the best interests of the child.
- *Denial by distance.* Mother has sole custody by an Oklahoma court order; father has two months of visitation during the summer. Mother and child have moved to New Hampshire. Father telephones mother in New Hampshire, as required by the court order, to give her advance notice for a

scheduled three-week visit during the summer. Mother says, "Go ahead; fly up here and waste your money on the airplane. We won't be here!" Father files an action for contempt.

SCOPE OF LAWYER'S INVOLVEMENT

Although the initial custody case is often quite complex and entangled, the visitation denial case, by comparison, is usually quite simple because it is either a motion for contempt or a motion to enforce the previous order. In initial custody cases, there are several factors to be presented, with the single focus on the child's best interests in the future. In visitation denial cases, on the other hand, although the central focus is still on the child, the task is to demonstrate how the previously ordered custody arrangement has affected the child's present condition. In a sense, the visitation denial stage is typically an expression of the failure of the initial custody stage.

When the client is the plaintiff at the visitation denial stage, there will be two major substantive issues to discuss at the first session with the client: (1) what has been the visitation pattern prior to the denial, and (2) why visitation was denied. Because the client has not seen the child, who is the most important issue, the effect of the denial cannot be discussed. Clients in visitation denial cases can readily describe the effects on themselves, but this is not the issue.

When the client is the defendant at the visitation denial stage, there are two basic topics of discussion between the custodial parent and the lawyer: (1) has visitation been denied, and (2) why. In either situation, the lawyer must rely almost entirely on his or her client's perceptions about what is going on.

The factual base for the noncustodial parent's case of denied visitation is simple. Here is the previous order of the court regarding visitation, and here are the times that visitation has been denied. Lay witnesses can document that the visitation has been denied, but they cannot opine the effects on the child. The custodial parent's position is then presented, and the rest is up to the judge.

As definitive as the lawyers may be in presenting the case, the judge has only his or her own insights into the nature of the real problem. Will a finding of contempt resolve the problem and re-establish the child's relationship with the denied parent? Will a dismissal of the matter make the problem go away, or will the same issue come back to court at a later date? What is needed is an understanding of the dynamics operating underneath the surface. Often what is needed is the involvement of a mental health professional who can delve into the problem using a therapeutic design.

In a situation in which one parent might be playing a visitation game, the attorney for the other parent should consider petitioning the court to appoint a social worker to investigate the situation. The professional intervention may indicate it is the lawyer's own client needing to change behavior or attitude, and this may appear to work against the client's interest. But it is the child who will be advantaged by the parent's change in behavior, and this in turn may create a more positive relationship between them.

SCOPE OF SOCIAL WORKER'S INVOLVEMENT

At the visitation denial stage, the social worker can be of great value on two levels. First, the social worker can attempt to see what interpersonal dynamics are at work between the child and the parents. The social worker can often view a set of circumstances through the de-emotionalized lenses of behavior.

- Who is doing what to whom and under what circumstances?
- What responses are produced in the people involved?
- What emotional triggers remain active from the marriage?
- What dependencies are in need of discarding, and what facets of independence need developing?
- What repetitive behaviors elicit what responses from the former spouse?
- Does the child resent being passed between the parents?
- Does the child wish for the reunion of his birth family?
- Are feelings of split loyalty taking shape?
- How does the child view life at the visitation home compared with the custodial home?

After review of the family history and interviews with the parents, a social worker could compile a list of questions. A compilation of questions would form the basis on which the social worker could begin to assess the problem.

Second, the social worker might begin to formulate a corrective plan for the visitation problem. Perhaps only some minor adjustments are required. Remove father's girlfriend from father's house on visitation days, and the child's feeling of isolation might disappear. Rearrange mother's visitation times to fit more readily into her work schedule, and the child might stop complaining that mother is always too tired. Sometimes, all it takes is a minor shift in time and people scheduling to develop the corrective plan.

The corrective plan[26] may require major rearrangements in some cases. Attitudes may have to change. As most mental health professionals know, this is no small task. It is suggested the custody evaluator have access to the child at both parents' homes and to all previous confidential reports. Also, it is suggested the

---

[26]The corrective plan can be a modification of visitation or even a modification of custody. As allowed by Rhode Island's statute regarding noncompliance with visitation, "upon a finding by the court that its order for visitation has not been complied with, the court shall exercise its discretion in providing a remedy, and define the noncustodial parent's visitation in detail. However, if a second finding of noncompliance by the court is made, the court shall consider this to be grounds for a change of custody to the noncustodial parent" (R.I. Gen. Laws § 15-5-16(d) (2008)).

evaluator be appointed by the court to investigate the full scope of the custody–visitation arrangement. Although suggested for many visitation cases, it is usually required for interstate visitation problems.

Upon first accepting the court appointment, the social worker should meet with both lawyers to discuss the scope and time frame of the investigation. It is important that each lawyer convey to his or her respective clients the purpose of the social worker's involvement. Trust is an important factor for success.

PRACTICAL TECHNIQUES

A court-appointed social worker can use the following techniques in a denial of visitation case:

- interview the custodial parent and obtain his or her version of the cause of the problem
- interview the noncustodial parent and obtain his or her version of the cause of the problem
- set up and monitor a visitation—actually experience the transfer of the child between the parents
- interview an older child regarding the visitation you have just monitored
- create a tentative hypothesis with respect to the problem
- test your hypothesis by changing conditions
- create a system of visitation modification and suggest it to the parents—if they are unreceptive, present it to the court.

A lawyer can use various strategies. If representing the custodial parent and the child does not want to visit, the lawyer should send the child to a social worker for confirmation that the problem lies with the child's relationship with the noncustodial parent and not with your client. This will eliminate the swearing contest between the lawyer's client and the noncustodial parent regarding who is at fault. It may also be the basis for expert testimony at trial.

If a lawyer is representing the visiting parent, he or she should petition the court to appoint a social worker to conduct a custody evaluation to assess the current arrangement and recommend any changes that may be helpful for the child. If the custodial parent objects to the selected professional, the lawyer should ask the court to select an evaluator from names supplied by both attorneys.

Some common visitation "games" the custodial parent plays to frustrate the noncustodial parent are as follows:

- *Visitation roulette.* When the visitation parent goes to see the child, the child is sometimes there and sometimes not there. The custodial parent gives no reason for the child's absence. The result is that the child has no regularity of parenting time with the visitation parent.

- *Free babysitter.* Any time the custodial parent wants to go out, the visitation parent is called, sometimes on an hour's notice. The visitation parent, feeling that any time with the child is precious, usually accepts the offer.
- *No pay no see.* The court-ordered visits are denied merely because child support is late. (Legally, there is no justification for withholding or denying visitation because of nonpayment of child support.)
- *Head trip.* The custodial parent repeatedly tells the child that the visitation parent is a bad person in hopes that the child will not want to go on visits. The extreme version of this game may lead to parental alienation whereby the child comes to believe the alienated parent is a bad person and wants to end all visits with that parent. Parental alienation can occur when divorcing parents transform a child into a relationship weapon by engaging in patterns of behavior designed to destroy the child's psychological connection with the other parent (Schacht, 2000).
- *Sick again.* Every time the visitation parent comes to visit the child, the child is sick.
- *Guilt trip.* The custodial parent says to the visitation parent, "I really don't know why the child doesn't want to see you; it must be because you broke up our marriage and walked out on me. I try to encourage the child to go with you, but he doesn't want to go."
- *Do it my way.* The custodial parent says to the visitation parent, "You can see my child this weekend if you take him to the zoo, then take him out to lunch, then buy him shoes, then bring him home sharply at six in the evening."
- *Nobody home.* The child never seems to be home when visitation is scheduled to begin. Even when the custodial parent is home, the child is always at a friend's house.
- *Something else to do.* The custodial parent always seems to arrange something "really neat" for the child to do during scheduled visitation times.
- *Live as I say.* The custodial parent tells the visitation parent, "Certainly you can have the child visit with you—just as soon as you get rid of your girlfriend, stop drinking beer and smoking cigars, and start using seatbelts."

These and many other games are played over a period of time, with varying effects on the child. Sometimes out of frustration, the visitation parent stops attempting to exercise the visitation rights. Later, when the visits are attempted again, the custodial parent denies contact with the child on grounds that "the child doesn't know who you are; you haven't visited him in so long."

The typical recourse for denial of visitation is the filing of a motion for contempt. It is suggested not to file such a motion on the basis of a one-time event, but to wait to see if a pattern develops. A less adversarial approach might be to file a motion to enforce the previous court order. With either approach, the issue of denial can be resolved either by the settlement process or by court intervention.

4

Custody Modification Stage

DEFINITION AND TIME FRAME

Custody modification means any change in the child's custody or visitation.[27] It applies to sole custody, joint custody, shared custody, or any other arrangement, whether the initial custody was by agreement or judicial determination.

Anytime after the initial custody award and until the child becomes emancipated constitutes of time frame for the custody modification stage. If the court modifies custody because of denial of visitation, then the custody modification stage continues. In most states, the courts can modify custody at anytime, but there are statutory time restraints in some states.[28] In many states,[29] a change in circumstances is required to modify custody.

---

[27]A more formal definition is found in the Uniform Child Custody Jurisdiction and Enforcement Act of 1997: "Modification means a child custody determination that changes, replaces, supersedes, or is otherwise made after a previous determination concerning the same child, whether or not it is made by the court that made the previous determination" (Section 102 (11). Since the UCCJEA Act has been enacted in all but two states, the definition of "custody modification" is essentially same throughout the country, whereas it is referenced by 48 different statutes. For example, Idaho passed the Act into law in 2000 (Id. Code. § 32-11-102(k) and Delaware passed the Act into law in 2002 [13 Del. Code. § 1902(11)]

[28]For example, Minnesota's statute sets forth six conditions that control custody modification, two of which are time periods of one or two years after the initial custody order was issued (Minn. Stat. § 518.18(d) (2006)). Also Ky. Stat. § 403.340(1) (2006) and Wis. Stat. § 767.325(1)(b)2 (2008) both provide for custody modification after two years and a substantial change in circumstances. Also, in Delaware, modification rules differ between initial cases that settled and those that were litigated. Del. Code § 729 (b) and (c).

[29]Pennsylvania's Supreme Court abolished the requirement in 1988. See *Karis v. Karis*, 544 A.2d 1328, 1331–1332 (Pa. 1988).

SOCIAL WORK INTERVENTION

The scope of social work intervention at the custody modification stage is enormous. The issue of whether or not to change the child's custody suggests the need for an assessment of the individual, social, and family situations. The child's present circumstances provide the social–environmental matrix for using several social work skills.

The child has been living with one parent and visiting with the other. This arrangement was either agreed to by the parents or imposed upon them by the court. The noncustodial parent is seeking to reverse the situation on grounds that the child's emotional well-being is deteriorating. Unless the custody is changed, the noncustodial parent argues, the child's continued custody–visitation arrangement will be devastating to the child's future. The custodial parent responds by either defending the child's present situation as adequate or accusing the noncustodial parent of enticing the child to change homes with a variety of promises.

Often one parent does not know what is really going on at the other parent's house. There are no longer any common friends between them, so there is no social connection to keep them informed. Either parent or both parents may be remarried. The in-laws who were once an integral part of their extended family life are now out of the picture.

Access to how each parent is living comes only from the child, and the child's version may be what the child thinks one parent wants to hear about the other. Some children even intentionally lie. The old feelings and accusations about which parent is better for the child (emotions popular at the initial stage) reappear with the same vigor as they did the first time—sometimes more so!

In custody modification cases, there is a great need for information about the child's feelings regarding each parent, as well as feelings about the various stepparents, step or half siblings, and other family members. Knowledge of child growth and development is often lacking—yet it is so important! What may be troublesome for a child at a younger age may not affect an older child.

Joint legal custody modifications are just as complex. The shared-time and shared-decisions phenomenon can create more problems for the child than he or she can handle. The need for a social worker at the custody modification stage is crucial if the court is to have sufficient evidence to make a determination.

CASE EXAMPLES

Custody modification cases are as varied as the families involved. The circumstances under which the children live are as different as the children themselves. Two cases with similar circumstances but different ages of children may require a different mental health intervention. Only the most general guidelines can be developed. Whether or not a substantial change in circumstances is required,[30] the custody evaluator should collect data regarding the current circumstances of the child. Events and changes in the life of one child might be of minor significance, whereas the same events in the life of another child might be devastating. The following case examples are offered to indicate the diversity of circumstances where social workers as custody evaluators are needed.

- *Child's preference.* Mother and father have been divorced for five years. Mother has sole custody, and father has visitation on alternate weekends and in the summer. The boy is 13 years old, and the girl is 14 years old. It is September, and the children have returned from a four-week visit with their father. During the summer, the boy told his father on numerous occasions that he wanted to live with him during the school year. When the father asked his daughter, she said "Yes. That would be fun." On several recent telephone calls, the boy reminded his father, so the father filed for modification. The daughter, however, began aligning herself with her mother and refused to talk to her father on the telephone. The father petitioned the court to appoint a custody evaluator to investigate.
- *Integration into new family.* Mother and father divorced two years ago, and father was awarded custody of their then six-year-old daughter. Mother has remarried; father has not. Mother married a single father with an eight-year-old daughter. The mother's natural daughter has become integrated into her new family, spending most of her visitation time with her new stepsister. Mother petitions for modification because she can now provide the child with a two-parent environment.
- *Psychological report.* Mother has custody of a 10-year-old son. Father has exercised his visitation rights religiously for two years. Father took the boy to a psychologist, who issued a report that identified the boy as a "youngster at risk under his present home life situation."
- *Cohabitation in custodial home.* Mother was awarded custody of two children, ages nine and 11 years. Mother's boyfriend has recently moved into mother's home. Father is a minister in an adjacent town. He petitions the court for custody modification and alleges that the immoral circumstances in mother's home are adversely affecting the welfare of his children.
- *Child refuses to visit the noncustodian.* Child is 14 years old and living with his father by a previous custody agreement. The child has refused to visit his mother on several occasions. Previous court action for denial of

---

[30]In those states where a substantial change in circumstances is required, it must be shown that the changed circumstances are linked to the child's welfare. For example, North Carolina appellate case law holds that "before a child custody order may be modified, the evidence must demonstrate a connection between the substantial change in circumstances and the welfare of the child, and flowing from that prerequisite is the requirement that the trial court make findings of fact regarding that connection" (*Carlton v. Carlton*, 145 N.C. App. 252 at 262, 549 S.E.2d 916 at 923 (2001)).

visitation found the father in contempt and resulted in several visits with the mother. After several visits, however, the child again refused to visit his mother. Father petitions the court to modify the visitation schedule and asks the court to appoint a custody evaluator to propose a modified visitation schedule.

SCOPE OF LAWYER'S INVOLVEMENT

In some states, the lawyer for the noncustodial parent seeking to modify custody has the twofold burden of showing (1) there have been substantial changes in the circumstances of the child since the case was in court before; and (2) these circumstances are having, and will continue to have, a detrimental effect on the child's welfare. The lawyer for the custodial parent will want to show the court that the circumstances are minor or at least correctable and that the change of custody itself will be detrimental to the child.

The "substantial change in circumstances" requirement has a long history in both statute and case law. The belief was that changing custody usually has a negative impact on the child of divorce, and therefore should be cautiously applied by trial courts. An explanation of this belief was written as early as 1955 in *Milim v. Mayfield*:

> Frequent hearings as to the custody of minor children of divorced parents should be frowned upon by courts and are not to be encouraged. A judgment as to such custody is *res judicata* as to the best interests of the children and such judgment should not be modified except upon a showing of changed conditions since the judgment, requiring, in the best interests of such children, that the custody be changed. The burden of proof is upon the party seeking such change to allege, offer proof and secure an affirmative finding from the trier of facts that conditions have so changed since the prior adjudication as to require a change of custody. (285 S.W.2d at p. 858)

In the 1970s, following the belief that modification typically has a negative impact on the child of divorce or separation, some states developed a two-part rule for custody modification. For example, in 1973, the Delaware legislature enacted a two-part rule for custody modification, one rule for cases less than two years old and another rule for cases older than two years:

- If the initial custody order was a consent order, then it can be modified anytime the Court finds that it is in the "best interest" of the child. (Del. Code § 729 (b))
- If the initial custody order was entered by the Court after a full hearing and it has been *less than two years* since it was entered, the order can be

changed only if the Court finds that continuing to enforce the order would endanger the child's physical health or significantly impair the child's emotional development. (Del. Code § 729 (c)(1))

- If the order was entered by the Court after a full hearing and it has been *more than two years* since it was entered, the order can be modified only after the Court considers all three of the following factors: (a) whether any harm caused by modifying the order is outweighed by the benefit of modifying the order; (b) each parent's compliance with the prior order; and (c) the "best interest" of the child. (Del. Code § 729 (c)(2)) If either attorney obtains a social worker to investigate the situation, that social worker would be hard-pressed to offer an opinion on custody modification unless there was access to both sides of the case.

Given the importance of "changed circumstances" in a custody modification case, one lawyer might suggest to the other lawyer that the parents stipulate that a social worker investigate the effects of the alleged changed circumstances on the child. This would provide both attorneys with independent data about the child's situation. The by-product of the social worker's involvement may mean that the case would settle out of court. The report issued by the stipulated social worker would be delivered to both attorneys, and either could call the social worker as an expert witness if the case did go to trial.

If one lawyer thought it was a good idea to involve a particular social worker, but simply opposed the one suggested, perhaps the two attorneys could agree on another social worker. There is a tendency to believe that the first person to contact a professional has some kind of advantage with him or her, even though this is not true with most professionals.

There might be a case in which one of the attorneys suggests the use of a social worker and the other attorney suggests a different professional. In this situation, both attorneys are giving credence to the need for professional involvement. One solution might be to petition the court for a conjoint appointment naming both professionals as custody evaluators.

Another alternative might be to petition the court to appoint a professional of its own selection. If this approach is used, there should be some suggestion made to the court as to the particular type of professional sought. The lawyer should clarify for the professional (or professionals) the state's legal definition of modification and distinguish it from initial custody.

SCOPE OF SOCIAL WORKER'S INVOLVEMENT

The social worker's role in custody modification is singularly aimed at assessing the effect of the present arrangement on the child and recommending changes, if any, that would best serve the child's interests. To understand the child's present situation, there should be a thorough review of background material. (This is similar to obtaining a social history in most mental health fields.) The better the understanding of the child's past, the better would be the understanding of the child's present situation.

In dealing with the attorneys, the social worker should be able to integrate his or her own professional perspective into the legal milieu that undergirds the case. For example, if custody modification is sought on grounds the child has become integrated into the noncustodian's family, this might indicate to the social worker that a social assessment and family evaluation might be needed. But, unlike the assessment in non-court-related studies, this assessment should be viewed in terms of whether or not the child's integration into the other family is detrimental to the child's welfare. Social integration into two families may provide the child with a superior childhood, as is argued by some joint custody advocates.

Generally, attorneys are needed at the beginning of the social worker's evaluation and again after the report has been completed. In between is the time when the evaluator's assessment is underway. During this time, there should be contact with the attorneys only regarding procedural matters related to the professional's assignment. Disclosure of any of the substantive content of the assessment to one attorney and not the other may be considered bias. *Ex parte* communication may be considered grounds for dismissal of the social worker's court appointment.[31]

Whether the social worker has come into the case by stipulation between the parties or by court order, if the case goes to trial the report will become the basis of his or her testimony. The social worker may be called as an expert witness by either side and be subject to cross-examination by the other side (and by the judge).

PRACTICAL TECHNIQUES

The court-appointed social worker should conduct a thorough assessment. Details of this assessment are discussed below.

- *Review the file.* The case file should be reviewed as soon as possible. The file is available from the clerk of the court. If the social worker has legal questions, then he or she should seek clarification by meeting (or having a telephone conference) with both attorneys. The professional should *not* contact the judge.

---

[31]*Ex parte* is a Latin legal term meaning from (by or for) one party. Some states have specific rules restricting communication between the evaluator and one attorney. For example, Cal. Fam. Code § 216(a) (2006) states "there shall be no ex parte communication between the attorneys for any party . . . and any court-appointed or court-connected evaluator." Also, ex parte communication is restricted by Rule 4.4 of the *Model Standards of Practice for Custody Evaluation* (Association of Family and Conciliation Courts, 2006) and by Standard I.B-3 of the *Model Standards of Practice for Child Custody Evaluation* (NASW Oregon Chapter, 2005).

- *Confidential releases.* Confidential releases should be signed by both parents. Even with signed releases, there may be limits on what information is obtainable, depending on the jurisdiction. It is a good idea to have a provision placed in the evaluator's appointment order stating that "both parties shall sign any release of confidential information forms as may be presented to them by the evaluator."
- *Records.* The following records might be obtained: previous reports used in the initial custody case; school records of the children; any recent professional reports; any records presented to the evaluator by the parents or their attorneys.
- *Interview with parents.* Each parent should be interviewed separately, beginning with the plaintiff, if possible. Some questions should be prepared in advance on the basis of the review of the file. Adequate time should be scheduled and parents should be allowed to ask questions about the evaluation procedure. These initial interviews can be either in an office or in the parents' homes when the children are not in the same room.
- *Interview with child.* The child, if of sufficient age or if the child's past statements are important, should be interviewed at home or at school. Office interviews with some children may not produce a basis of trust, so another neutral location may be more comfortable for them.
- *School.* If the child is in school, the teachers, guidance counselor, or other school personnel should be interviewed.
- *Observations in both homes.* The child should be observed at both the custodial home and the noncustodial home. Have the child give you a "tour" at both houses. Every effort should be made to spend an equal amount of time in both homes. Observations can be unstructured or structured with specific assignments or projects useful in assessing parenting styles (Hynan, 2003).
- *Reference people.* Obtain from each parent the names and telephone numbers of several reference people who have observed the parent–child interactions in the past. These collateral individuals might be useful to either support or refute personal observations.
- *Testing.* If testing appears appropriate, it should be done after the first contact with the child. The tests selected should have some bearing on previous factors involved in the case. The professional may have to answer in court the question of why each test was selected.
- *Reflection.* Take time to think about the data collected, and seek out other data if appropriate before writing a report.
- *Conference with parents.* In some cases, before writing the report, it may be useful to schedule a conference with both parents present to discuss with them your tentative position regarding your views.
- *Conference with attorneys.* After the custody report has been issued, have a conference with the attorneys so the issues might be narrowed. Your report might be instrumental in leading to a settlement. If the case goes to

trial, you may learn what portions of the report they believe are most important and those they believe are the weakest. This could be quite useful information when preparing for your testimony.

The lawyer can assist the court-appointed social worker. Under some circumstances, the lawyer can provide the social worker with a summation of issues believed to be at the heart of the case. The lawyer can help your client provide a list of reference people. In addition, he or she can convince your client to be fully cooperative with the social worker who is conducting the custody evaluation. Finally, the attorney should let the social worker know that he or she is available for procedural issues, if needed.

When the client wants to modify custody, the lawyer can be helpful by conducting a thorough interview with your client to determine the specific circumstances that have changed since the last custody order. The lawyer can maintain a focus on how those changes are affecting the child. Also, the lawyer can have the client take the child to a professional to measure how the present custody arrangement is affecting the child. In some jurisdictions, this procedure may or may not be allowed without the consent of both parents. If the professional concludes there are detrimental effects, then the lawyer can seek out lay witnesses who can provide concrete examples of the professional's conclusions.

5

Child Removal Stage

DEFINITION AND TIME FRAME

As presented here, *child removal* means taking the child or children out of the state of jurisdiction to parts known or unknown. The removal may be with permission or without permission, and the removal may be by the custodial parent or by the noncustodial parent.

Child removal with permission is called "relocation"[32] in most states. Child removal without permission is called "parental kidnapping," or "child abduction," or "child snatching," or "family abduction." *Family abduction* is defined as

> the taking, keeping, or concealing of a child or children by a parent, other family member, or person acting on behalf of the parent or family member that deprives another individual of his or her custody or visitation rights. (Hoff, 2002, p. ix)

The child removal stage has no particular time frame. Child removal by either parent may occur at any time during or after the initial custody stage. Typically, however, removals (relocations or abductions) occur after the modification stage of custody.

---

[32]A relocation case in California is called a "move away" case. Relocation cases are subject to different legal burdens in different states. Also, there are many definitions of child removal and civil and criminal statutes vary among the states.

SOCIAL WORK INTERVENTION

The scope of social work intervention at the child removal stage can be the most profound of all the previous stages of custody. What is at issue here usually affects the child's entire life, as well as the child's extended family. Removal of the child from the state creates for the child a new social life and a new environment. When the child's home, school, friends, and family (the child's roots) are disrupted by the removal, the child is most at risk. The scope of mental health intervention at this stage may sometimes call for psychotherapeutic intervention.

When the custodial parent petitions to relocate with the child, the noncustodial parent may file a petition opposing the move. Some states are guided by case law,[33] and other states have statutory factors[34] that instruct the courts how to rule in relocation cases. Therefore, social workers should conduct evaluations consistent with the guidelines operative in the particular state. Florida's statutory relocation factors are typical of several other states.

(a) The nature, quality, extent of involvement, and duration of the child's relationship with the parent proposing to relocate with the child and with the non-relocating parent, other persons, siblings, half-siblings, and other significant persons in the child's life
(b) The age and developmental stage of the child, the needs of the child, and the likely impact the relocation will have on the child's physical, educational, and emotional development, taking into consideration any special needs of the child
(c) The feasibility of preserving the relationship between the non-relocating parent . . . through substitute arrangements
(d) The child's preference [if mature]
(e) Whether the relocation will enhance the general quality of life for both the parent seeking the relocation and the child
(f) The reasons . . . for seeking or opposing the relocation
(g) Whether . . . the proposed relocation is necessary to improve the economic circumstances of the parent . . . seeking relocation
(h) That the relocation is sought in good faith
(i) The career and other opportunities available
(j) A history of substance abuse or domestic violence
(k) Any other factor affecting the best interest of the child. (Fla. Stat. Ann. § 61.13001(7) (2008))

---

[33]For example, in California, *In re Marriage of Burgess*, 913 P.2d 473 (1996), and *Baures v. Lewis*, 770 A.2d 214 (2001). Both are state supreme court cases.

[34] Some states have few statutory relocation factors (Utah, for example, has only three factors: Utah Code Ann. § 30-3-37(4)(a–c) (2008)) and other states have many (Alabama, for example, has 16 factors: Ala. Code § 30-3-169.3(a)(1–16) (1975 (1998 Supp.)).

In a relocation case in Florida, the social worker as custody evaluator can assist the court by collecting data relative to these statutory factors. With regard to (f), the reasons for seeking or opposing relocation is the most commonly found factor in those states that have enacted statutory relocation factors. The issue here is motive:

- What is the underlying motive on the part of the parent seeking to relocate, or the underlying motive of the parent opposing the proposed relocation?
- Is the parent petitioning for permission to relocate doing so out of spite, or out of a sincere effort to weaken or breach the child's relationship with the other parent?
- Is the parent seeking to block the relocation doing so merely to burden the other parent with unnecessary litigation costs?

Louisiana enacted a provision allowing the court to impose a sanction on a parent proposing a relocation of the child or objecting to a proposed relocation of a child if it determines that the proposal was made or the objection was filed for any of the following reasons: (a) to harass the other parent or to cause unnecessary delay or needless increase in the cost of litigation; (b) the case is based on a frivolous argument; or (c) the case is based on allegations without supportive evidence (La. Rev. Stat. § 355.16 (1997)).

If the custodial parent in a state without statutory or case law factors petitions the court to relocate with the child, the role for the social worker, if appointed as a custody evaluator, should be to evaluate three things: (1) the child's present social, emotional, education, and physical environment; (2) the proposed new custodial environment; and (3) the child's "readiness" for such a move.

When either the custodial or the noncustodial parent removes the child to parts unknown, obviously no direct services can be provided to the missing child until located. Once located, however, the child may be in need of individual therapy. Family counseling is almost always beneficial for the returned child and one (or both, if possible) parents. In some cases, depending on the events and experiences during the kidnap period, psychotherapy or psychiatric treatment has been needed.

If the custodial or the noncustodial parent removes the child in violation of a previous court order, the full range of mental health services may be needed, depending on the specific situation of the individual child. The social worker might be in the best position to advise the court regarding which services would be most appropriate for the child.

CASE EXAMPLES

Child removal cases in many ways are broader than other custody cases because the concern is usually a comparison of two environments, one familiar to the child and the other either not as familiar or totally unknown to the child. The following child removal examples are divided into those called relocation and those called child abduction.

Relocation

Employment. Mother and father divorced two years ago, and mother received sole custody by consent in Michigan. Father has fully exercised his visitation, and the child has a positive relationship with him. Mother has been working as a teaching assistant at the local college and taking classes in the evening toward a doctoral degree. In three months, she expects to receive the degree and has been offered a teaching position at a Florida university. The child is eight years old and well adjusted to his school and community. The father knew of the mother's intentions to eventually leave Michigan, but nothing was mentioned about it in their consent order that gave the mother custody. The mother files a petition to relocate to Florida, and the father files an answer opposing the move.[35]

Remarriage. Father and mother have joint legal and physical custody of two children, ages 12 and 15 years, as a result of a California court order. Mother is single and father is engaged to a lawyer in Philadelphia. Parenting time is divided equally on an alternating weekly basis, and holidays and summers are also equally divided. Father files a petition to relocate to Philadelphia with the children and proposes that the mother have parenting time for two consecutive months every summer. Mother files an answer seeking sole custody.[36]

Family. In a custody modification case in Boise, Idaho, father and mother were awarded joint custody of their eight-year-old son. Mother petitions the court for permission to relocate with the boy to Spokane, Washington, to be closer to her large extended family. She alleges the father's family in Boise consists of only an older sister whereas her family in Spokane consists of 14 family members. Under Idaho law, there is a presumption against relocation, so the mother would have the burden of showing that the move would be in the boy's best interests.[37]

Health. Mother and father live in Topeka, Kansas. They share joint custody of their three daughters, ages two, four, and six years. Father has had asthma all

---

[35]In Michigan, the relocating parent (that is, the mother) has the burden of proof under *Grew v. Knox* (694 N.W.2d 772 (2005)). The custody evaluator appointed in this case should be familiar with Mich. Comp. Laws Ann. § 722.31(4) (2008).

[36]Under California law, the nonrelocating parent has the burden of proof because there is a presumption in favor of relocation (see *In re Marriage of LaMusga*, 88 P.3d 81 (2004) and Cal. Fam. Code § 7501 (2006)).

[37]*Roberts v. Roberts*, 138 Idaho 401; 64 P.3d 327 (2003). Because Idaho has no statutory relocation factors, the social worker would be obliged in the custody evaluation to collect data pertaining to the statutory factors for best interests, as set forth in Idaho Code § 32-717(1) (2006).

his life, and the six-year-old has recently been diagnosed with asthma. He filed a timely notice to relocate to Arizona with the children, alleging the climate in Arizona would be more conducive to his and his oldest daughter's condition. Mother filed an objection that argued against the proposed move.[38]

Religion. A Jewish couple divorced in Durango, Colorado, and mother was awarded sole custody of their nine-year-old son. Father was awarded alternate weekend visitation from Friday after school until Sunday night. Father filed a custody modification action when the boy was 11 years old; the case settled with father increasing his visitation periods to three weekends each month. Now, father files for relocation because he wants his son to have a bar mitzvah, but there are no synagogues in Durango. The Colorado Supreme Court has ruled that relocation in that state is neither favored nor opposed.[39]

Child Abduction

The rescue. Mother has sole custody, and father visits every other weekend. Mother works in a bar near a military base. On many weekends when he picks up his son, father finds different men in "intimate" association with mother. Also, he has frequently observed drugs in her apartment. On several occasions, when he has returned his son, mother was not at home. He would stay with the boy at mother's next door neighbor's apartment until she returned. Through this neighbor, father has learned that the police have been to mother's apartment on at least five occasions. On one Friday evening, when father picked up his son, he found a large bruise on the boy's arm. The son said, "One of mommy's friends hurt me." Father immediately took the boy to the police and, on their advice, took him to the hospital. After the boy's arm was treated, he and father left the hospital and have not been seen since.

The intimidation. Mother files for custody, and father contests it. Mother is required to bring the child, age three years, to court for the hearing. On the way to the hearing, father stops by mother's house and shows her some photographs of her in compromising situations with her lesbian lover. Father tells mother that his lawyer hired a detective without his consent, and that his lawyer was going to have the detective testify about the photographs. Mother tells father she will pick up their child at day care and will meet him at the courthouse for the custody hearing scheduled for that afternoon. She picks up the child, but does not appear at the courthouse. The whereabouts of mother and child are still unknown.

---

[38]Citing Kan. Stat. Ann. § 60-1620(c) (2007), she argued the effect the proposed move would have on her rights.

[39]*In re Marriage of Ciesluk*, 113 P.3d 135 (Colo. 2005), courts are guided by the eleven statutory factors listed in Colo. Rev. Stat. Ann. § 14-10-129(2)(c), (d) (2008).

SCOPE OF LAWYER'S INVOLVEMENT

The lawyer's involvement with relocation cases is basically the same as involvement with other custody modification cases. A motion for appointment of a social worker or other professional might be the first step, whether the lawyer is representing the parent seeking to relocate to another state or the parent resisting the move. In either case, it is important to obtain some information about the new home that is being proposed for the child.

Not all states have the same burden of proof regarding relocation.[40] On the one hand, in Alabama there is a presumption that relocation is not in child's best interests. The relocating parent bears the initial burden of proof. If that burden is met, the burden then shifts to the parent opposing the relocation (see Ala. Code § 30-3-169.4 (1998)). On the other hand, in Alaska there is a presumption that relocation is in the child's best interests, as long as the reasons for relocating are legitimate. Thus, the burden of proof rests on the side of the parent opposing relocation (see *Moeller-Prokosch v. Prokosch*, 2001).

The attorney representing the parent petitioning to relocate the child to a new state will need to have information about the positive features of the proposed new home and its environment for the child. The attorney representing the parent attempting to block the relocation will also need information about the proposed new home. The client probably will be more concerned with losing his or her child than the actual proposed new home. To bring information to the court about the proposed custodial environment in the new state, the attorney might want to recommend the court appoint a social worker to investigate the situation.

One attorney will want to demonstrate that the proposed new community will be beneficial for the child and will enhance the child's general welfare. The other attorney will want to demonstrate that the child's present community is responding well to the child's needs. In either case, a court-appointed custody evaluator would be in a good position to gather the available information without favoring one side or the other at the onset.

In a child abduction case, the role of the lawyer is often complicated because it may involve federal and international laws. Nonetheless, at a minimum, the lawyer should be familiar with the Uniform Child Custody Jurisdiction and Enforcement Act of 1997 (UCCJEA) and its enactment in his or her state. This is a uniform state law designed to deter interstate parental kidnappings and promote the uniform application of jurisdiction and enforcement provisions in interstate child custody and visitation cases. Forty-six states and the District of Columbia have enacted the UCCJEA into their state laws. As of April 2009, only Massachusetts, Missouri, New Hampshire, and Vermont remain; all four states have bills pending in their legislatures.

---

[40]In 15 states, there is a presumption that relocation will serve the child's best interests, so the burden of proof to the contrary rests with the other parent. In eight states there is no presumption one way or the other. In most of the remaining 27 states, the burden rests with the parent seeking relocation.

The role of the custody evaluator is often more complicated at this stage when the child has been removed without permission of the other parent or the court. Statutes differ regarding parental abduction, and social workers as custody evaluators should become familiar with the relevant statutes. For example, the North Carolina statutes have provisions for the return of a child or the enforcement of a previous custody determination (N.C. Gen. Stat. § 50A-3 (2008)), whereas the New Jersey statutes boldly proclaim (and have since 1948) that children of divorce shall not be removed without consent or cause:

> When the Superior Court has jurisdiction over the custody . . . of the minor children of parents divorced, separated or living separate, and such children are natives of this State, or have resided five years within its limits, they "shall not be removed out of [the State] . . . without the consent of both parents, unless the court, upon cause shown, shall otherwise order." (N.J. Stat. Ann. § 9:2-2 (1948, 2008))

In a child abduction case, the lawyer representing the parent seeking to find the child might find it appropriate to ask the court to appoint a guardian *ad litem* (GAL) for the benefit of the missing child. Some of the guardian's duties might be to:

- locate the child by using the legal status of GAL to contact local, state, and federal authorities, including embassies
- evaluate the conditions under which the child was taken
- evaluate the current lifestyle of the child where the child is found
- obtain the child's own feelings about the removal
- recommend to the court the best future custody–visitation arrangement for the child.

Some states require that GAL be an attorney,[41] but most states do not. For example, South Carolina Code: § 63-3-820(A) (2008) reads: "A guardian ad litem may be either an attorney or a layperson." An experienced social worker who has been appointed as a custody evaluator might be well suited to this position. The GAL would be appointed to conduct a custody evaluation. Theoretically, this is when the roles of a neutral evaluator and a child advocate would blend.

If the noncustodial parent abducted the child, the motion to appoint a GAL would be made by the custodial parent. If the custodial parent abducted the child, the motion to appoint a GAL would be made by the noncustodial parent. In either case, notice to the "missing" parent would not be required because the

---

[41]See, for example, Oklahoma: "In any proceeding when the custody or visitation of a minor child or children is contested by any party, the court may appoint an attorney at law as *guardian ad litem* upon motion of the court or upon application of any party to appear for and represent the minor children" Okla. Stat. § 43-107.3 A.1 (2007)).

appointment of a GAL is a nonadversarial action; neither party's rights are in jeopardy. In all states, the court can make a *sua sponte* order by appointing a GAL on the court's own motion. For example, New Jersey's Rules Governing Practice in the Chancery Division, Family Part, states this explicitly: "A *guardian ad litem* may be appointed by the court on its own motion" (Rule 5:8B(a) [2000]).

SCOPE OF SOCIAL WORKER'S INVOLVEMENT

Relocation

The social worker's involvement in a relocation case should be obtained through a formal appointment from the court of the home state jurisdiction. If a parent intends to remove the child to another state, then the appointed social worker will have some formal authority to obtain information on the proposed conditions and facilities in the new state.

An appointment order from one state may not be binding on individuals and agents in other states, but it may provide some clout for the appointee's investigation. For example, when one of the parents has stated an intention to take employment in another state such as in the example mentioned earlier, the prospective employer may be reluctant to share with the custody investigator the details of the job offer. However, if an appointment order is presented, that employer might provide the evaluator with details of the contract offer. If a contract has been offered, then the employer is probably serious about wanting to hire the parent. Consequently, it would be logical that the employer might be more willing to cooperate with the evaluator.

If the parent alleges that down payment on a house has been made in the new state, the realtor may hesitate to discuss the proposed sale. Presentation of the appointment order might produce a copy of the real estate sales agreement.

Child Abduction

When the social worker is going to be involved in an abduction case, it is suggested the appointment be as a GAL for the missing child. This role is sufficiently broad to assist the professional in locating the missing child and in acting as the child's advocate in any forthcoming litigation. Agencies such as law enforcement, credit card companies, banks, insurance companies, airlines, moving companies, public utilities, telephone companies, and others may provide information to a GAL, but not to a custody evaluator.

The relationship between guardian and ward is similar in nature to the relationship between attorney and client. It is a protective relationship. This needs to be carefully explained to the missing parent and to the child (depending on the child's age) when found. The GAL does not represent either parent; the guardian represents the child's interests. In child custody cases, the child is also legally considered a "real party in interest." Describing of the role and responsibilities of a GAL, one judge wrote (*Clevenger v. Clevenger*, 1983):

> The court finds that . . . the children in this matter are also "real parties in interest" and have definite interest in this litigation. To attribute any less status to the children is to lose sight of the meaning of "the best interest of the child" . . . consequently, it is not imperative that standing be limited to the parents in custody matters. The *guardian ad litem* has the responsibility to serve the best interests of the children who are his protective wards, and in that capacity he may file in their behalf, and appeal orders in their behalf, and perform other duties toward the protection of their interests. (Superior Court of King County, Washington, # D119731, 1983)

PRACTICAL TECHNIQUES

Relocation

When the custodial parent seeks court permission to remove the child and relocate another state, how can the social worker determine whether the intended move is in the child's best interests? What criteria can be used to evaluate the intended move?[42]

- *Motive.* Basic to the issue of the custodial parent being permitted to remove the child from the state is the question of motive. Is the custodial parent merely attempting to relocate to get away from the other parent? Have visitations been disruptive or uncomfortable for the parent or for the child? Is the motive for relocation an attempt to frustrate the child's visitation with the noncustodial parent out of spite or anger? Is the motive for relocation retaliation for the other parent contesting custody in the first place? The basic issue here is whether the petition for relocation is custodian centered or child centered?
- *Advantages for the child.* Will the proposed removal to another state be advantageous to the child's general welfare? Are there specific health, educational, social, religious, emotional, or familial advantages to the relocation that would benefit the child? What are they?

---

[42]In recent years, many states have created statutory guidelines their courts must consider in resolving relocation issues. Some of these states are Ariz. Rev. Stat. § 25-408(J) (2007); Colo. Rev. Stat. § 14-10-129 (2008); Fla. Stat. § 61.13(2)(d) (2008); Ind. Code § 31-17-2.2-1(b) (2006); Iowa Code § 598.21.D (2008); La. Rev. Stat. § 9:355.1 (2008); N.D. Cent. Code § 14-09-07 (2007); Ohio Rev. Code § 3109.051(G)(1) (2008); and Tenn. Code Ann. § 36-6-108 (2008). Some of the states without statutory guidelines regarding relocation are Alaska Stat. § 25.24.150(c) (2008); Del. Code Ann. tit. 13, § 722(a) (2005); Tex. Fam. Code § 153.133 (2008); and Wash. Rev. Code Ann. § 26.09.405 (2008).

- *Proposed visitation.* Does the custodial parent seeking the relocation have a proposed visitation schedule that will adequately substitute for the current visitation schedule? Does the proposed substitute parenting plan provide the child with a similar or better relationship with the noncustodial parent? What is the proposed plan?
- *Reason for resisting.* What are the reasons why the noncustodial parent resists the proposed relocation? Are these reasons adult centered or child centered? Has there been an attempt to negotiate a new visitation schedule that will permit the move? Is the attempted blockage being conducted out of spite or out of a real concern for the child? What, specifically, are the reasons for resisting the relocation of the child?
- *The child's view.* Does the child have a particular desire to stay or to go? What is the child's view? How will the proposed relocation affect the child's welfare in terms of the child's current involvement with family, school, community, and other factors? Of course, the age and maturity of the child should be an important consideration.

Child Abduction

There is frequently an important role for a social worker in a child abduction case after the child has been located and returned. The child may need what is called "reunification therapy." A judge may want a professional to provide services to the child to help reunite the child with the parent from whom the child was taken. In some cases, the parent who abducted the child will be awarded restructured parenting time or supervised visitation under the custody doctrine—"Don't punish the child for parental misconduct."

There may also be a role for the social worker in a child abduction case before the child has been located. Here, the professional may be appointed as the child's GAL. In a few states, such an appointment is reserved for a licensed attorney,[43] but in most states, the appointment is left up to the discretion of the court.

In some states, the GAL may conduct an investigation, and the court can specify its scope. For example, in West Virginia,

> In its discretion, the court may order a written investigation and report to assist it in determining any issue relevant to proceedings under this article. The investigation and report may be made by the *guardian ad litem* [and the] court shall specify the scope of the investigation or evaluation and the authority of the investigator. (W.Va. Code Ann. § 48-9-301(a) [2008])

When a social worker is appointed as the child's GAL, the authority over the appointment is retained by the court having jurisdiction over the custody matter.

---

[43] For example, Mo. Rev. Stat. § 210.160 (2008) and Va. Code § 16.1-266(A) (2008).

If the appointment order can be registered in another state, then that state is required to give "full faith and credit" to the order. Services provided by a GAL are different from those services described by the social worker's state license.

Some of the techniques that a GAL might use to locate the missing child are listed below.

- Under the federal law known as the Family Educational Rights and Privacy Act of 1974 (FERPA),[44] the GAL can find out whether school records have been transmitted to another school. The GAL is the child's representative and has the same educational rights as the parent. Schools that do not comply with FERPA requirements are subject to loss of federal funding. If school records have been transferred, the guardian is entitled to have the name, address, and telephone number of the new school.
- If the GAL has reason to believe that a family member assisted in the abduction of the child, or knows the current location of the child, the guardian should register his or her appointment order in the state where that family member resides. Then, the GAL might institute a legal action against the family member as a co-conspirator. The action might be a civil tort or a criminal warrant. Sometimes, positive results can occur by merely suggesting to the family member that the GAL intends to institute legal action.
- In some situations, it might be wise to make an application for the appointment of an attorney for the GAL.
- The GAL might report the child abduction to the district attorney of the county from which the child was abducted. District attorneys can enter felony warrants into the National Crime Information Center.[45]
- There may be reason to contact military agencies if the child's abductor is currently or has ever been in one of the armed services.[46]

---

[44]Family Educational Rights and Privacy Act of 1974 (20 U.S.C. § 1232g) gives parents and guardians certain rights with respect to their children's education records. The law applies to all schools that receive funds under an applicable program of the U.S. Department of Education. (Contact: Family Policy Compliance Office, U.S. Department of Education, 400 Maryland Avenue, SW, Washington, DC 20202-5920; phone: 202-260-3887.)

[45]The National Crime Information Center is a computerized index of criminal justice information (that is, criminal record history information, fugitives, stolen properties, and missing persons) that is maintained by the FBI. It is available to federal, state, and local law enforcement agencies, and other criminal justice agencies. It is operational 24 hours a day, 365 days a year. (Contact: National Crime Information Center, 1000 Custer Hollow Road, Clarksburg, WV 26306; phone: 304-625-2000.)

[46]The four service addresses are U.S. Army, Personnel Service Support Center, 8899 East 56th Street, Fort Benjamin Harrison, IN 46249-5301; U.S. Air Force, HQ AFPC/DPDXIDL, 550 C St. West Ste. 50, Randolph AFB, TX 78150-4752; U.S. Navy, Bureau of Naval Personnel, PERS 312F, 5720 Integrity Drive, Millington, TN 38055-3120; U.S. Marine Corps, Commandant of the Marine Corps, Headquarters USMC, Code MMSB-10, Quantico, VA 22134-5030.

Conclusion

The five stages of custody have been discussed from the respective roles of the lawyer and the social worker. Each stage has been defined in terms of its time frame, and practical techniques have been offered along with case examples.

Social workers are well suited to conduct custody evaluations because many of the values and standards of the profession of social work are consistent with the values courts expect of custody evaluators. Evaluators should make clear to all individuals involved in the evaluation that their role is not to advocate for any party in the litigation, but to assist the court in determining what is best for the child. Many of the values of the custody evaluator are consistent with the values embodied in the standards set forth in the NASW *Code of Ethics* (2008):

Custody evaluators should understand the role of culture in the beliefs and behaviors of those being evaluated. This is consistent with the NASW code:

> Social workers should understand culture and its function in human behavior and society, recognizing the strengths that exist in all cultures. (Standard 1.05[a])

Custody evaluators should be neutral professionals and offer impartial judgments based on the sum total of data available. This is consistent with the NASW code:

> Social workers should be alert to and avoid conflicts of interest that interfere with the exercise of professional discretion and impartial judgment. (Standard 1.06[a])

Custody evaluators should not use their position to exploit others or to further their own interests. This is consistent with the NASW code:

> Social workers should not take unfair advantage of any professional relationship or exploit others to further their personal, religious, political, or business interests. (Standard 1.06[b])

Custody evaluators should not engage in professional relationships with anyone involved with the custody evaluation. This is consistent with the NASW code:

> Social workers should not engage in dual or multiple relationships . . . . (Standard 1.06[c])

Custody evaluators should seek advice from other experts regarding topics where their own expertise is limited. This is consistent with the NASW code:

> Social workers should seek consultation only from colleagues who have demonstrated knowledge, expertise, and competence related to the subject of the consultation. (Standard 2.05[b])

Custody evaluators should take care to retain all notes and records obtained during the course of the custody evaluation. This is consistent with the NASW code:

> Social workers should take reasonable steps to ensure that documentation in records is accurate and reflects the services provided. (Standard 3.04[a])

Custody evaluators should not allow their personal problems to interfere with their performance or their judgment. This is consistent with the NASW code:

> Social workers should not allow their own personal problems . . . to interfere with their professional judgment and performance. . . . (Standard 4.05[a])

Given the similarity between many of the values expected in custody evaluation work and those articulated in the NASW *Code of Ethics*, it would appear that social workers would be well suited for this work. Although custody work can be challenging, it can also be extremely rewarding. When custody decisions are right, the children will benefit; but when custody decisions are wrong, the children can be damaged. The importance of child custody determinations is undisputed. Chief Justice Frank D. Celebrezze of the Ohio Supreme Court said it this way: "[S]tatutes can be amended and case law can be . . . overruled, [but] children grow up only once. When a mistake is made in a custody dispute, the harmful effects are irrevocable." (*In Re Wonderly*, 67 Ohio St. 2d 178 at 188; 423 N.E.2d 420 at 427 (Ohio 1981)).

Custody evaluation work definitely can be challenging, but it can also be extremely worthwhile. Social workers have an excellent opportunity to provide a valuable service to the courts and to make an important difference to children and their families caught up in the confusion and, sometimes, hostilities of contested child custody disputes.

Appendix A

Custody Evaluations by Social Workers[47]

Case	Citation	State/Year	Social Worker
Wilker v. Buse	10/1/08	(Iowa App. 2008)	Susan Gauger
Connelly v. Connelly	169 P.3d 1279	(Or. App. 2007)	Billie Bell
Aronow v. Aronow	725 N.W.2d 659	(Iowa App. 2007)	Ann McDonald
Luplow v. Luplow	924 So.2d 1135	(La. App. 2006)	Leigh Ann O'Brien
Dykes v. McMurry	938 So.2d 330	(MS App. 2006)	Deslie Bonano
Fernandez v. Pizzalato	902 So.2d 1112	(La. App. 2005)	Michael McNeil
Henry v. Henry	904 So.2d 800	(La. App. 2005)	Diane Carroll
Dawson v. Heath	A04-1988	(Minn. App. 2005)	Michael Weinstein
Gould v. Gould	ADR-2000-360	(Mont. Dist. 2005)	Donna Hale
Peters v. Costello	891 A.2d 705	(Pa. 2005)	Najma Davis
Marriage of Cooksey	Dec. 14, 2005	(Or. 2005)	Mazza
Wyman v. Wyman	FA030733009	(Conn. Super. 2004)	Celeste Senechal
Kilpela v. Kilpela	2003 MN 591	(MNCA. 2003)	Robert Jokela
Marriage of McCord	Nov. 26, 2003	(Iowa App. 2003)	Sandra Pelzer
In re Dexter S.	2003 CA 797	(CACA. 2003)	Charles Herbelin
Arneson v. Arneson	670 N.W.2d 904	(S.D. 2003)	Judy Zimbelman
Berg v. Berg	2002 N.D. 69	(N.D. 2002)	James Davis
Downey v. Muffley	767 N.E.2d 1014	(Ind. Ct. App. 2002)	Nanette Fredericks
Stone v. Glass	35 S.W.3d 827	(Ky. App. 2000)	Unnamed
Perry v. Magic Valley	995 P. 2d 816	(Id. 2000)	Susan DeHaan
Kirby v. Fox	526 S.E.2d 19	(W.Va. 1999)	Unnamed
Gill v. Dufrene	706 So.2d 518	(La. App. 1997)	Charlotte Fornea

---

[47]These are some of the reported cases that reached the appeal level.

Case	Citation	State/Year	Social Worker
Marriage of Abrahamson	924 P.2d 1334	(Mont. 1996)	Donna Hale
Patronas v. Patronas	693 So.2d 469	(Ala. Civ. App. 1996)	Nancy DeVaney
Marriage of Cupples	531 N.W 2d 656	(Iowa App. 1995)	Unnamed
Bradshaw v. Bradshaw	891 P.2d 506	(Mont. 1995)	Karen Emerson
Larson v. Larson	888 P.2d 719	(Utah App. 1994)	Unnamed
Custody of J.M.D.	857 P.2d 708	(Mont. 1993)	Donna Hale
Haryick v. Haryick	828 P.2d 769	(Alaska 1992)	Unnamed
Merriam v. Merriam	799 P.2d 1172	(Utah App. 1990)	John Bagley
Pikula v. Pikula	374 N.W.2d 705	(Minn. 1985)	Nancy Archibald
Ebnet v. Ebnet	347 N.W.2d 840	(Minn. 1984)	Unnamed

Appendix B

Custody Statutes

Ala. Code § 30-3-131, § 30-3-133, § 30-3-152, § 30-3-132 (1975) (1998 Supp.)
Alaska Stat. § 25.24.150, § 25.20.090 (2006)
Ariz. Rev. Stat. Ann. § 25-403, § 13-3601 (2007)
Ark. Code Ann. § 9-15-215, § 9-13-101 (2008)
Cal. Fam. Code § 3044, § 3011, § 3020, § 3080, § 3040, § 3190, § 3191, § 3192 (2006)
Colo. Rev. Stat. Ann. § 14-10-124 (2008)
Conn. Gen. Stat. Ann. § 46b-56a (2008)
Del. Code. Ann. tit. 13 § 705A, § 722, § 706A (2005)
D.C. Code § 16-914 (2008)
Fla. Stat. Ann. § 61.13 (2008)
Ga. Code Ann. § 19-9-1, § 19-9-3 (2008)
Haw. Rev. Stat. Ann. § 571-46 (2007)
Idaho Code § 32-717B, § 32-717 (2006)
Illinois 750 Ill. Comp. Stat. 5/101 *et. seq.* (2000)
Ind. Code Ann. § 31-17-2-8 (Burns, 2006)
Iowa Code Ann. § 598.41, § 236.5 (2008)
Kan. Rev. Stat. Ann. § 60-1610 (2007)
Ky. Rev. Stat. Ann. § 403.270 (2006)
La. Rev. Stat. Ann. § 9:364, § 9:335, La. Civ. Code Ann. art. 132 (2008)
Me. Rev. Stat. Ann. tit. 19-A § 1653, § 1657 (2006)
Md. Code Ann. Fam. Law § 9-101.1–9-307 (2008)
Mass. Gen. Laws Ann. chs. 208 § 31A, 209 § 38, 209C § 10 (2007)
Mich. Comp. Laws Ann. § 722.23 (2008)
Minn. Stat. Ann. § 518.17, § 257.025 (2006)

Miss. Code Ann. § 93-5-24 (2005)
Mo. Ann. Stat. § 455.050, § 452.375 (2008)
Mont. Code Ann. § 40-4-212 (2007)
Neb. Rev. Stat. § 42-364 (2008)
Nev. Rev. Stat. Ann. § 125C.230, § 125C.220, § 125.480, § 125.490 (2007)
N.H. Rev. Stat. Ann. § 458:17 (2008)
N.J. Stat. Ann. § 9:2-4 (2008)
N.M. Stat. Ann. § 40-4-9.1 (2008)
N.Y. Dom. Rel. Law § 240(1)(a) (2008)
N.C. Gen. Stat. § 50-13.2 (2008)
N.D. Cent. Code § 14-09-06.2 (2007)
Ohio Rev. Code Ann. § 3109.04 (2008)
Okla. Stat. Ann. tit. 43 § 112.2, § 110.1, tit. 10 § 21.1 (2007)
Or. Rev. Stat. § 107.137 (2008)
23 Pa. Cons. Stat. Ann. § 5303 (2008)
R.I. Gen. Laws § 15-5-6 (2008)
S.C. Code Ann. § 63-3-530 (2008)
S.D. Codified Laws § 24, § 25, § 26 (2008)
Tenn. Code Ann. § 36-6-101, § 36-6-106, § 36-6-406 (2008)
Tex. Fam. Code § 153.004, § 153.131, § 153.134 (2008)
Utah Code Ann. § 30-3-10.2, § 30-3-10 (2008)
Vt. Stat. Ann. tit. 15 § 665 (2008)
Va. Code Ann. § 20-124.3 (2008)
Wash. Rev. Code Ann. § 26.09 (2008)
W.V. Code Ann. § 48-9-201, § 48-9-205, § 48-9-209, § 48-9-207 (2008)
Wis. Stat. § 767.401-481 (2008)
Wyo. Stat. Ann. § 20-2-201 (2007)

Appendix C

Mental Health Professions

Educators
National Education Association
1202 16th Street, NW
Washington, DC 20036-3290
http://www.nea.org/index.html

Marriage & Family Counselors
American Association for Marriage
   and Family Therapy
112 South Alfred Street
Alexandria, VA 22314-3061
http://www.aamft.org

American Family Therapy Academy
1608 20th Street, NW, 4th Floor
Washington, DC 20009
http://www.afta.org

Pastoral Counselors
American Association of
Pastoral Counselors
9504-A Lee Highway
Fairfax, VA 22031-2303
http://www.aapc.org

Psychologists
American Board of Professional
   Psychology
600 Market Street
Suite 300
Chapel Hill, NC 27516
http://www.abpp.org

American Psychological Association
750 First Street, NE
Washington, DC 20002
http://www.apa.org

School Guidance Counselors
American Counseling Association
5999 Stevenson Ave.
Alexandria, VA 22304
http://www.counseling.org

Social Workers
National Association of Social Workers
750 First Street, NE, Suite 700
Washington, DC2002
http://www.naswdc.org

National Organization of Forensic
    Social Work
460 Smith Street, Suite K
Middletown, CT 06457
http://NOFSW.org

Sociologists
American Sociological Association
1307 New York Avenue, NW #700
Washington, DC 20005
http://www.asanet.org

References

Ala. Code § 30-3-169.4 (1975) (1998 Supp.)

American Academy of Child and Adolescent Psychiatry. (1997). *Practice parameters for child custody evaluation. Journal of the American Academy of Child and Adolescent Psychiatry, 36*(10 Suppl.), 9. Washington, DC: Author.

American Academy of Psychiatry and the Law. (2005). *Ethics guidelines for the practice of forensic psychiatry.* Bloomfield, CT: Author.

American Psychological Association. (1994). Guidelines for child custody evaluations in divorce proceeding. *American Psychologist, 49,* 677–680.

Association of Family and Conciliation Courts. (2006). *Model standards of practice for child custody evaluation. Family Court Review, 45*(1), 70–91.

Clarwar, S. (1982). One house, two cars, three kids. *Family Advocate, 5*(2), 14–17.

Clevenger v. Clevenger, No. D119731 (Superior Court of King County, Washington, 1983)

Dalton, C., Drozd, L., & Wong, F. (2006). *Navigating custody and visitation evaluations in cases with domestic violence: A judge's guide.* Reno, NV: National Council of Juvenile and Family Court Judges.

Fehnel v. Fehnel, 186 N.J. Super. 209, 452 A.2d 209 (App. Div. 1982).

Ga. Code Ann. § 19-9-3 (3)(O) (2008).

Gladwell, M. (2005). *Blink.* New York: Little, Brown.

Goode, W. (1956). *After divorce.* New York: Free Press.

Govern, P. (2004, April 2). Brooks discusses social work and the law. *Reporter: Vanderbilt Medical Center's Weekly Newspaper*, p. 4.

Hoff, P. M. (2002). *Family abduction—Prevention and response* (5th ed.). Alexandria, VA: National Center for Missing and Exploited Children.

Hynan, D. J. (2003). Parent–child observations in child custody evaluations. *Family Court Review, 41*, 214–223.

Kass, A. (1998). Clinical advice from the bench. *Child Adolescent Psychiatric Clinics of North America, 7*, 247–258.

Keesee v. Keesee, 675 So.2d 655 (Fla. 5th D.C.A. 1996).

Louisiana State Board of Social Work Examiners. (1998). *Guidelines for child custody evaluations.* Baton Rouge: Author.

Luftman, H., Veltkamp, L. J., Clark, J. J., Lannacone, S., & Snooks, H. (2005). Practice guidelines in child custody evaluations for licensed clinical social workers. *Clinical Social Work Journal, 33*, 327–357.

Marsden, P. (2005, February 12). Speed thinking: A review of "Blink" by Malcolm Gladwell. *New Scientist*, p. 48.

Martin v. Martin, 132 S.W.2d 426 at 428. (1939).

Milim v. Mayfield, 285 S.W.2d 852 (Tex. Civ. App. 1955).

Moeller-Prokosch v. Prokosch, 27 P.3 314 (Alaska 2001).

Mont. Code Ann. § 40-4-224(4) (2007).

National Association of Social Workers. (2008). *Code of ethics of the National Association of Social Workers.* Washington, DC: NASW Press.

National Association of Social Workers, Oregon Chapter. (2005). *Model standards of practice for child custody evaluations.* Portland: Author.

Schacht, T. E. (2000). Prevention strategies to protect professionals and families involved in high-conflict divorce. *University of Arkansas at Little Rock Law Review, 22*, 565–592.

Skafte, D. (1985). *Child custody evaluations: A practical guide.* Beverly Hills, CA: Sage Publications.

Uniform Child Custody Jurisdiction and Enforcement Act of 1997. (Proposed legislation by the National Conference of Commissioners on Uniform State Laws in Chicago)

Woody, R. H. (1978). *Getting custody: Winning the last battle of the marital war.* New York: Macmillan.

Bibliography

Stage 1—Marital Discord

Ahrons, C. (1994). *The good divorce: Keeping your family together when you marriage comes apart*. New York: Harper Perennial.

Amato, P. R. (2001). Children of divorce in the 1990: An update of the Amato and Keith (1991) meta-analysis. *Journal of Family Psychology, 15*, 355–370.

Amato, P. R., & Sobolewski, J. M. (2001). The effects of divorce and marital discord on adult children's psychological well being. *American Sociological Review, 66*, 900–921.

Arnold, W. (1977). *Divorce: Prevention or survival*. Philadelphia: Westminster Press.

Atkin, E., & Rubin, E. (1976). Breaking up. In *Part-time father: A guide for the divorced father* (pp. 51–61). New York: New American Library.

Beck, D. F. (1976). *Marriage and the family under challenge*. New York: Family Service Association of America.

Bohannan, P., & Bernard, J. (1971). The six stations of divorce. In P. Bohannan (Ed.), *Divorce and after* (pp. 33–62). New York: Doubleday.

Eisler, R. T. (1977). *Dissolution*. New York: McGraw-Hill.

Hetherington, E. M., & Kelly, J. (2002). *For better or for worse: Divorce reconsidered*. New York: Norton.

Holden, G. W., Geffner, R., & Jouriles, E. N. (Eds.). (1998). *Children exposed to marital violence: Theory, research, and applied issues*. Washington, DC: American Psychological Association.

Hunt, M. (1979). The unmaking of marriages. In *Divorce experience* (pp. 30–35). New York: New American Library.

Kaslow, F. W. (1984). Divorce: An evolutionary process of change in the family system. *Journal of Divorce, 7*, 21–39.

Knox, D. (1971). *Marriage happiness.* Champaign, IL: Research Press.

Knox, D., & Schacht, C. (2008). *Choices in relationships* (9th ed.). New York: Thomson/Wadsworth.

Krantzler, M. (1975). *Creative divorce.* New York: New American Library.

Madden, R. G. (1998). *Legal issues in social work, counseling and mental health.* Thousand Oaks, CA: Sage Publications.

Palisi, B. J. (1984). Symptoms of readiness for divorce. *Journal of Family Issues, 1*, 70–89.

Rofes, E. E. (Ed.). (1982). *The kids book of divorce.* New York: Random House.

Rosner, S., & Hobe, L. (1974). Why marriages break down. In *The marriage gap* (pp. 86–108). New York: McGraw-Hill.

Stith, S. M., Green, N. M., Smith, D. B., & Ward, D. B. (2008). Marital satisfaction and marital discord as risk markers for intimate partner violence: A meta-analytic review. *Journal of Family Violence, 23*, 149–160.

Young, L. R. (1973). *The fractured family.* New York: McGraw-Hill.

Stage 2—Initial Custody

Sole Custody

Ackerman, M. (1996). The MMPI-2 in child custody evaluations. *American Journal of Family Law, 4*, 1–11.

Association of Family and Conciliation Courts. (2008). *Ten tips for interviewing children in custody evaluations: Ask the experts.* Madison, WI: Author.

Bieland, D., & Lemmon, J. (1977). *Social work and the law.* St. Paul, MN: West Publishing.

Bienenfeld, F. (1987). *Helping your child succeed after divorce.* Claremont, CA: Hunter House.

Derdeyn, A. (1975). Child custody consultation. *American Journal of Orthopsychiatry, 45*, 791–801.

Druckman, J. M. (1977). Application to child custody determination. *Family Coordinator, 26*, 451–458.

Goldenberg, R. (1998, January). Practical aspects of parenting conflicts: Preparing parents for litigation. *Florida Bar Journal, 72*(1), 54–60.

Gozansky, N. (1976). Court ordered investigations in custody cases. *Williamette Law Journal, 12*, 511–526.

Heinze, M. C., & Grisso, T. (1996). Review of instruments assessing parenting competencies used in child custody evaluations. *Behavioral Sciences and the Law, 14*, 293–313.

Hynan, D. J. (2003). Parent–child observations in child custody evaluations. *Family Court Review, 41*, 214–223.

Kelly, J. B. (1994). The determination of child custody in the USA. *Future of Children, 4*, 121–142.

Maccoby, E. E., & Mnookin, R. H. (1992). *Dividing the child: Social and legal dilemmas in custody.* Cambridge, MA: Harvard University Press.

Warshak, R. A. (1996). Gender bias in child custody decisions. *Family and Conciliation Courts Review, 34*, 396–409.

Warshak, R. A. (2000). Blanket restrictions: Overnight contact between parents and young children. *Family and Conciliation Courts Review, 38*, 422–445.

Woody, R. H. (1978). *Getting custody.* New York: MacMillan.

Joint Custody

Bauserman, R. (2002). Child adjustment in joint-custody versus sole-custody arrangements: A meta-analytic review. *Journal of Family Psychology, 16*, 91–102.

Ernst, T., & Altis, R. (1981, December). Joint custody and co-parenting: Not by law but by love. *Child Welfare, 60*, 669–677.

Garner, J. R. (2007). Where's the morph: Joint custody vs. the changed circumstances rule. *Journal of Contemporary Legal Issues, 16*, 277–283.

Greif, J. B., & Simring, S. K. (1982). Remarriage and joint custody. *Conciliation Courts Review, 20*, 9–14.

Ilfield, F. W., Ilfield, H. Z., & Alexander, J. R. (1982). Does joint custody work? A first look at outcome date relitigation. *American Journal of Psychiatry, 139*, 62–66.

Most, C. W. (2007). It's time for a joint custody presumption. *New York Family Law Monthly,* 8(7), 1.

Perrow, C. (2003). The origin and evolution of Florida's presumption against rotating custody: A guideline for Florida judges. *Florida State University Law Review, 30*, 503–526.

Ricci, I. (1980). *Mom's house, dad's house: Making shared custody work.* New York: MacMillan.

Roman, M., & Haddad, W. (1978). *The disposable parent: The case for joint custody.* New York: Holt, Rinehart & Winston.

Salfi, D. J., & Cassady, N. (1981, June). Who owns this child? Shared parenting before and after divorce. *Conciliation Courts Review, 20*, 31–40.

Steinman, S. (1981). The experience of children in a joint custody arrangement: A report of a study. *American Journal of Orthopsychiatry, 51*, 403–414.

Stage 3—Denial of Visitation

Atkin, E. L., & Rubin, E. (1976). The visiting father. In *Part-time father: A guide for the divorced father* (pp. 62–82). New York: Vanguard Press.

Boland, M. L. (2001). *Your right to child custody, visitation and support.* New York: Sphinx.

Braver, S. H., Wolchlk, S. A.. Sandler, I. N., Gogas, B. S., & Zvetina, D. (1991). Frequency of visitation by divorced fathers: Differences in reports by fathers and mothers. *American Journal of Orthopsychiatry, 61,* 448–454.

Johnston, J. R. (1992). *High conflict and violent parents in family court: Findings on children's adjustment and proposed guidelines for the resolution of custody and visitation disputes* [Final Report]. San Francisco: Judicial Council.

Kelly, J. B., & Wallerstein, J. S. (1977). Part-time parent, part-time child: Visiting after divorce. *Journal of Clinical Child Psychology, 6,* 51–54.

Koch, M.A.P., & Lowery, C. R. (1984). Visitation and the noncustodial father. *Journal of Divorce, 8,* 47–65.

Pollack, D., & Mason, S. (2004). Mandatory visitation: In the best interest of the child. *Family Court Review, 42,* 74–84.

Seagull, A. A., & Seagull, E. A. W. (1977). The non-custodial father's relationship to his child: Conflicts and solutions. *Journal of Clinical Child Psychology, 6,* 11–15.

Silver, G. A. (1981). *Weekend fathers.* New York: Harper & Row.

Turkat, I. D. (1997). Management of visitation interference. *Judges Journal, 36,* 17–47.

Victor, I., & Winkler, W. A. (1977). The visitation father. In *Fathers and custody* (pp. 126–135). New York: Hawthorn Books.

Stage 4—Custody Modification

Black, A. K. (2005). Florida Supreme Court defines "substantial change" in child custody modification proceedings. *Florida Bar Journal, 79*(10), 64–66.

Cohen, I. M. (1998). Postdecree litigation: Is joint custody to blame? *Family Court Review, 36,* 41–53.

Foster, H. H., & Freed, D. J. (1964). Modification of custody awards. *New York University Law Review, 39,* 622–626.

Franks, M. R. (1983). Changing custody. In *Winning custody* (pp. 115–120). Englewood Cliffs, NJ: Prentice-Hall.

Oliphant, R. E. (2000). Redefining a statute out of existence: Minnesota's view of when a custody modification hearing can be held. *Wm. Mitchell Law Review, 26,* 711–730.

Seem, S. J. (2004). Impact of No Child Left Behind on post-divorce custody modification. *Heinonline-University of Chicago Legal Forum,* p. 625.

Swenson, L. (1987). Factors contributing to the success of required mediation of child custody disputes. *Family Court Review, 25*(2), 49–53

Stage 5—Child Removal

Relocation

Austin, W. G. (2000). Relocation law and the threshold of harm. *Family Law Quarterly, 34*, 63–82.

Casasanto, M. D. (1978). Guardian ad litem: A proposal to protect the interests of children. *New Hampshire Bar Journal, 20*, 20–35.

Haberman, P. S. (2005). Relocation and protection for domestic violence victims in volatile divorce and custody situations. *Family Court Review, 43*, 149–163.

Handschu, B. E. (1985). Custodial removal: May a custodian leave the jurisdiction with the child? A review and recommendations. *Women's Rights Reporter, 8*, 247–266.

Kelly, J. B., & Lamb, M. (2003). Developmental issues in relocation cases involving young children: When, whether, and how? *Journal of Family Psychology, 17*, 193–205

McKenzie, P. A. (2006). Nowhere to run: Custody, relocation and domestic violence in Florida. *Nova Law Review, 31*, 355–374.

Mlyniec, W. J. (1977). The child advocate in private custody disputes: A role in search of a standard. *Journal of Family Law, 16*, 1–17.

Scholl, B. (2004). A matter the court should consider: The risk of relocation and the custody conundrum. *Journal of Law & Family Studies, 6*, 353–361

Turkat, I. D. (1999). Relocation as a strategy to interfere with the child–parent relationship. *American Journal of Family Law, 11*, 39–41.

Wallerstein, J. S., & Tanke, T. J. (1996). To move or not to move: Psychological and legal considerations in the relocation of children following divorce. *Family Law Quarterly, 30*, 305–332

Warshak, R. A. (2000). Social science and children's best interests in relocation cases: Burgess revisited. *Family Law Quarterly, 34*, 83–113.

Parental Kidnapping

Crouch, R. E. (2000). An intricate maze of child-snatching statutes. *Family Advocate, 23*(4), 29–33.

Gill, J. E. (1981). *Stolen children*. New York: Seaview Books.

Johnson, J. R., & Girdner, L. K. (1998). Early identification of parents at risk for custody violations and prevention of child abductions. *Family Court Review, 36*, 392–409.

Johnston, J. R., & Girdner, L. K. (2001). *Family abductors: Descriptive profiles and family interventions*. Washington, DC: Office of Juvenile Justice Prevention.

Katz, S. N. (1981). *Child snatching: The legal response to the abduction of children*. Washington, DC: American Bar Association Press.

Lewis, J. A. (1976). Legalized kidnapping of children by parents. *Dickinson Law Review, 80*, 305–327.

Lewis, K. (1978). Child snatching American style. *Children Today, 7*(6), 18–21, 35.

Lewis, K. (1979, February 3). Parental kidnapping: Some would make it a federal crime. *Chicago Tribune*, Tempo Sect., pp. 1–2.

Noble, D. N., & Palmer, C. E. (1984). The painful phenomenon of child snatching. *Social Casework, 65*, 330–336.

Reynolds, S. E. (2006). International parental child abduction: Why we need to expand custody rights protected under the child abduction convention. *Family Court Review, 44*, 464–483.

Reading Material for Selected Topics

Child Custody Evaluations

Association of Family and Conciliation Courts. (2006). Model standards of practice for child custody evaluation. *Family Court Review, 45*, 70–91.

Dalton, C., Drozd, L. M., Wong, F. Q. F. (2006). *Navigating custody and visitation evaluations in cases with domestic violence*. Reno, NV: National Council of Juvenile and Family Court Judges.

Gould, J. W., & Stahl, P. (2000). The art and science of child custody evaluations: Integrating clinical and mental health models. *Family and Conciliation Courts Review, 38*, 392–414.

Heilbrun, K. (2001). *Principles of mental health assessment*. New York: Kluwer Academic/Plenum Press.

Hynan, D. J. (1998). Interviewing children in custody evaluations. *Family and Conciliation Courts Review, 36*, 466–478.

Hynan, D. J. (2003). Parent–child observations in custody evaluations. *Family Court Review, 41*, 214–223.

Luftman, V. H., Veltkamp, L. J., Clark, J. J., Lannacone, S., & Snooks, H. (2005). Practice guidelines in child custody evaluations for licensed clinical social workers. *Clinical Social Work Journal, 33*, 327–357.

Otto, R. K., Edens, J. F., & Barcus, E. H. (2000). The use of psychological testing in child custody evaluations. *Family and Conciliation Courts Review, 38*, 312–340.

Pollack, D. (2003). Social workers as expert witnesses: What you should know. *ABA Child Law Practice, 21*, 190–191.

Sarnoff, S. (2004, Fall). Social workers and the witness role: Ethics, laws, and roles. *Journal of Social Work Values and Ethics, 1*, 1–17

Skafte, D. (1985). *Child custody evaluations—A practical guide*. Beverly Hills: Sage Publications.

Stahl, P. M. (1994). *Conducting child custody evaluations*. Thousand Oaks, CA: Sage Publications.

Stahl, P. M. (2000). Understanding child custody evaluation for parents. In *Parenting after divorce* (chapter 7). Atascadero, CA: Impact Publishers.

Take the stand: Primer for the expert witnesses. (1998, January). *NASW News*, p. 16.

Weissman, H. N. (1991). Child custody evaluations: Fair and unfair professional practices. *Behavioral Sciences and the Law, 9*, 469–476.

Parental Alienation

Bone, M., & Walsh, M. (1999). Parental alienation syndrome: How to detect it & what to do about it. *Florida Bar Journal, 73*(3), 44–47.

Bow, J. N., Gould, J. W., & Flens, J. R. (2009). Examining parental alienation in child custody cases: A survey of mental health and legal professionals. *American Journal of Family Therapy, 37*, 127–145.

Bruch, C. S. (2001). Parental alienation syndrome and parental alienation: Getting it wrong in child custody cases. *Family Law Quarterly, 35*, 527–552.

Clawar, S. S., & Rivlin, B. (1991). *Children held hostage: Dealing with programmed and brainwashed children.* Chicago: American Bar Association.

Darnall, D. (1998). *Divorce casualties: Protecting your children from parental alienation.* Lanham, MD: Taylor.

Gardner, R. (1972). *The parental alienation syndrome: A guide for mental health and legal professionals.* Cresskill, NJ: Creative Therapeutics.

Gardner, R. (2001). Should courts order PAS children to visit/reside with the alienated parent? A follow-up study. *American Journal of Psychology, 19*, 61–106.

Kelly, J. B., & Johnston, J. R. (2001). The alienated child: A reformulation of parental alienation syndrome. *Family Court Review, 39*, 249–266.

Lee, S. M., & Olesen, N. W. (2001). Assessing alienation in child custody and access evaluations. *Family Court Review, 39*, 282–298.

Schacht, T. E. (2000). Prevention strategies to protect professionals and families involved in high-conflict divorce. *University of Arkansas Little Rock Law Review, 22*, 565–592.

Stahl, P. M. (2003). Understanding and evaluating alienation in high-conflict custody cases. *Wisconsin Journal of Family Law, 24*, 20–26.

Stoltz, J. M., & Ney, T. (2002). Resistance to visitation: Rethinking child and parental alienation. *Family Court Review, 40*, 220–231.

Index

The letter "n" in page references denotes a footnote.

Virginia custody statutes, 24n14
visitation with noncustodial parent,
47–48

W
Washington custody statutes, 61n42
Weinhold, Barry K., 13n10

Wechsler Intelligence Scale for
Children, 26
West Virginia custody statutes, 15n13, 62
Wisconsin custody statutes, 27n18, 28n19
Wonderly, In Re, 66–67
Wong, F., 25
Woody, R. H., 14

About the Author

Ken Lewis, PhD, was a social work professor at several universities during the 1970s, and for the past 25 years he has been director of Child Custody Evaluation Services of Philadelphia. He has been court appointed as either guardian *ad litem* or child custody evaluator in more than two dozen states, and his specialties are interstate custody and high-conflict cases. He offers workshops on custody evaluations to social workers and can be reached by e-mail at DrKenLewis@snip.net.